Imaging the
WORD

Imaging the
WORD

An Arts and Lectionary Resource

Susan A. Blain, Editor
Sharon Iverson Gouwens
Catherine O'Callaghan
Grant Spradling

Volume 3

United Church Press

Cleveland, Ohio

Thomas E. Dipko	Executive Vice President, UCBHM
Audrey Miller	General Secretary, Division of Education and Publication
Lynne M. Deming	Publisher
Sidney D. Fowler	Editor for Curriculum Resources
Kathleen C. Ackley	Associate Editor for Curriculum Resources
Monitta Lowe	Editorial Assistant
Marjorie Pon	Managing Editor
Kelley Baker	Editorial Assistant
Susan Cash	Permissions Coordinator
Paul Tuttle	Marketing Director
Linda Peavy	Associate Marketing Director
Madrid Tramble	Production Manager
Martha A. Clark	Art Director
Angela M. Fasciana	Sales and Distribution Manager
Marie Tyson	Order Fulfillment/Inventory Control Manager

United Church Press, Cleveland, Ohio 44115
© 1996 by United Church Press
Imaging the Word has been designed to be used with *The Inviting Word: A Worship-centered, Lectionary-based Curriculum for Congregations* and with the New Revised Standard Version of the Bible. All scripture quotations, unless otherwise noted, are from the New Revised Standard Version of the Bible, © 1989 by the Division of Christian Education of the National Council of the Churches of Christ in the U.S.A. Adaptations have been made for clarity and inclusiveness. Used by permission.

Printed in Hong Kong on acid-free paper
First printing, 1996

Design: Kapp & Associates, Inc., Cleveland, Ohio
Cover art: George Tooker, *Embrace of Peace,* Hartland, Vermont. Used by permission of the artist.

Library of Congress Cataloging-in-Publication Data
(Revised for v. 3.)

Lawrence, Kenneth T. (Kenneth Todd), 1935–
Imaging the Word.

May be used in conjunction with "Word among us/The inviting word" Sunday School curriculum published by United Church Press.
Includes bibliographical references and index.

1. Church year. 2. Revised common lectionary. 3. Bible—Illustrations. 4. Bible—In literature.
5. United Church of Christ—Education. 6. United churches—United States—Education. 7. Reformed Church—United States—Education. 8. Christian education—Textbooks for adults—United Church of Christ. 9. Christian education—Textbooks for children—United Church of Christ. I. Weaver, Jan Cather, 1955– . II. Wedell, Roger William. III. Title.

BV30.L39 1994   263'.9   94–823

ISBN 0–8298–0970–8 (cloth : v. 1 : acid-free paper)
ISBN 0–8298–0971–6 (pbk. : v. 1 : acid-free paper)
ISBN 0–8298–1032–3 (cloth : v. 2 : acid-free paper)
ISBN 0–8298–1033–1 (pbk. : v. 2 : acid-free paper)
ISBN 0–8298–1085–4 (cloth : v. 3 : acid-free paper)
ISBN 0–8298–1086–2 (pbk. : v. 3 : acid-free paper)

Note: The editor and writers for volumes 2 and 3 are Susan A. Blain, Sharon Iverson Gouwens, Catherine O'Callaghan, and Grant Spradling.

Contents

Foreword

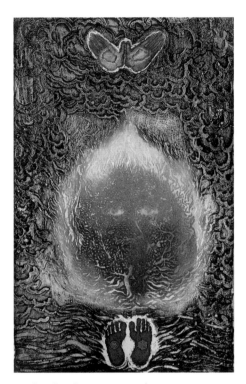

Paul Koli, *The Burning Bush*

Before God had a name, God was seen and heard in the desert bush that burned. God appeared in vivid reds and golds, in the blazing crackles and hisses, in the image. God was not the bush nor the flame, but through and in both, God was known. Moses saw and heard God.

Unless we recognize God when God reaches into this world, do we truly know the Holy One? Often we do not expect God to come into our world—even though here God has acted since the time of creation. Today one may recognize God in nature as Moses did, but God may also be discerned in an abundance of other images, including the media, the arts, and the experiences of daily living. We are wise not to mistake an image for God. We are careful not to assume the holy in every image. But unless we are attentive to the world around us, we proceed without gazing into any image at all. We may pass a burning bush from which God beckons us.

Imaging the Word assists individuals and congregations in the transforming, often difficult, discipline of discerning God in the world. This volume places inspired Scripture alongside the arts, which the church's tradition may or may not see as inspired. The juxtaposition of the two is intended to deepen one's knowledge of God and of the Bible by challenging us to connect faith with poetic and visual images. *Imaging* is also intended to challenge people to perceive God and the power of the Word of God when the book is closed, as one lives in the world. For these reasons the arts are central to *Imaging the Word*, a vital component of *The Inviting Word: A Worship-centered, Lectionary-based Curriculum for Congregations* (first developed with the name *Word Among Us*).

The arts—images in sound, sight, movement, and language—frame the experience of the world. Artists create, but they also define and limit. Artists choose what they include and exclude in their art. A photographer may shoot an image of the entire earth from space or a painter may focus on the detail of aging hands at prayer. A novelist may follow a family's saga from their ancient roots in Africa to contemporary life in an American city, while a poet describes a spider's web. Through the skill of the artist to frame, we focus on a very particular experience of the world. And the experience is *of* the world.

Look at any painting. Read any poem. Watch any television show. From what sources did the artist draw? From where did the sources come? The sources do not usually originate in museum galleries, cloistered libraries, symphony halls, or theaters, but rather from the world. The commonplace sources intervene from the external world of relationships, politics, economics, history, science, and religion; or well up from the internal world of emotions, dreams, insight, imagination, and faith. The source may be a word, a color, a sound, or a form. Whatever the source, it comes from living in and perceiving the world.

But how does one discern God in the overwhelming images in the world? How does one discern God while standing before a burning bush or a statue of a golden calf, looking at a magazine ad or a Monet, listening to Madonna or Mozart? To be prepared to discern God's presence

For each entry, *Imaging the Word* focuses on a Bible reading from the *Revised Common Lectionary*. The lectionary is a three-year cycle of systematic readings from Hebrew Bible stories, the Psalms, the Gospels, and other scriptures from the New Testament. These selected readings for each week and holy days assist congregations and parishes to prayerfully and imaginatively move through the Bible and the church year in their worship and study. Because *Imaging the Word* was created to enhance *The Inviting Word*, which begins in September, this volume begins with readings from Proper 17, Cycle A.

requires prayer, worship, study, and service. Through exploring the Bible, one may discover the images and ways of God. God is a god of creation, salvation, liberation, and incarnation. Guided by these acts of God, one may identify the same God in the world as found in the Word. Cognizant of those ways, we are better able to do as Richard Kearney suggests: "to discriminate between a liberating and incarcerating use of images, between those that dis-close and those that close off our relation to the other . . . those that communicate and those that manipulate."

Even when the images are secular as in the stunning photo of *Tomoko and Her Bath*, one may see, in a mother's embrace, God's steadfast love and tenderness for God's children (page 117). Read the testimony of Oseola McCarty in a newspaper and discover how God's generosity inspires generosity in God's followers (page 285). View a play or film and learn "Sometimes— there's God—so quickly!" as spoken by the manipulative and seductive Blanche when her spirit is broken by the brief kisses of the gentleman Mitch in *A Streetcar Named Desire*.

The community of faith assists one in the discernment as it forms itself around the biblical tradition. The community often guards against the idolatry or misperceptions of individuals. Yet one's own intimacy with God, guided by those biblical images and ways of God, may open one to declare, "Aha, in this God speaks!" even when the community may not hear or see.

The Bible readings and the arts in *Imaging the Word* provide an opportunity for individuals, groups, and congregations to engage in such discernment. Through individual prayer and meditation, through study and reflection at home or in groups, through use with the other resources from *The Inviting Word*, or through use in the ministries of a congregation, *Imaging the Word* will spark discussion of, exploration around, and questions about God's presence and action.

Often may God come along your way. And when God comes, may you recognize the Holy Living One.

* * *

I am grateful to Maria Harris who so carefully outlines a prayerful process for perceiving the arts in "That We May See: An Introduction." Her work along with the work of Kenneth T. Lawrence, the editor of the first volume of *Imaging the Word,* and that of the design firm Kapp & Associates has been foundational to the significance of the arts throughout all *The Inviting Word* resources. The article "Playing and Praying: Tips for Engaging Children with Art" by Susan Blain provides ways to assist children to be involved in the arts as they begin to discover God in the world. Sharon Iverson Gouwens, Catherine O'Callaghan, Grant Spradling, and Susan Blain worked together beautifully on this volume to assure a rich diversity of artistic form and theological insight.

Sidney D. Fowler
Editor for Curriculum Resources
United Church Press

That We May See: An Introduction

Ben Shahn, *The Red Staircase*

The great rabbi Abraham Heschel once lamented that our vision is impaired by negative habits of seeing—our inability to truly see. Instead of knowing what we see, we are all too prone to see only that to which we are accustomed. *Imaging the Word* is designed not only to alert us to this danger, but to enrich our seeing and to turn constricted habits of perception into broad sources of insight and wisdom. By combining poetry, prayer, music, and the visual arts, this powerful resource offers encounters with works that can convert patterns of superficial sight into profound understandings of what it means to live before God in a world of mystery and wonder.

To get a sense of how superficial seeing can become understanding, take a moment with Ben Shahn's *The Red Staircase* (page 240). What do you see? Perhaps you are attracted by the red of the stairway and the figure starting to climb it. If so, what do you notice about the climber? At first it may be only the solidity and slight hunch of his shoulders, or the fact that he is using crutches. But when you take a bit more time, you realize the man is missing one of his legs. Then you begin to be aware of the staircase itself, going up and going down, endless, leading to no apparent destination.

Max Beckmann, *Landscape, Cannes*

Lars Topelmann

Women in Namibia Dancing
(Afrapix/Impact Visuals, N.Y.)

Looking further, you find more. You note a half-hidden figure at the right of the painting, taking upon his shoulders a basket filled with shattered pieces of rock from what appears to be a landscape of broken rock. These remnants come, at least in part, from the crumbling building next to the staircase. And when your eyes rest on this second figure for a moment, you notice that a path seems to have been cleared by this stone-gatherer and that a distant horizon beckons. There is, after all, somewhere to go.

Much more lies in the picture, but already notice that your seeing has changed. It has become deeper and richer. Actually, it has turned into another kind of seeing that is more than simply visual; it has turned to the "I see" of understanding something you had not understood before, the "I see" of "I get it!" You realize now that the picture is open to interpretation. It has meaning. It speaks of journeys, and human work, and loss, and brokenness. It speaks of connectedness to earth and sky. It speaks of paths and of pathways. It speaks of time, including in this case its time of creation, 1944, when a terror-filled twentieth-century war was coming to an end. Shahn has told us that to him, the painting speaks of both the hope and the fate of humanity.

Paths and pathways abound in this volume. Max Beckmann's *Landscape, Cannes* (page 179), for example, recalls the procession of Jesus into Jerusalem. Yet even as it impels reflection on the last week of Jesus' life, it invites us—if we allow it to—to probe the comings and the goings of our own lives, and the entries into our own Jerusalems. The nave of Westminster Abbey (page 229) has a similar power to teach of paths and pathways as it evokes connectedness with all the naves of all the churches we have ever entered.

Imaging the Word is not only about these themes. It is about many more, such as joy and transformation. The leaping figure on the beach is joined in joy to the leaping, dancing figures of the women of Namibia (page 139), and both are candidates for the kind of transformation about which Alice Walker writes on page 151 and to which František Kupka's new vision can bid us (see page 150). Spending time to be with such works of art, to see them more fully, and to trust our interpretations of them, we are often stirred to respond. We may even ask, "Now that I have looked, and seen, and found meaning, is anything more required of me? Am I, as the ancient biblical text suggests, 'to do justice and to love kindness as I go humbly with God?'" (Micah 6:8).

A Process for Discovery

A simple process exists to guide us toward seeing what the arts might teach us and toward developing worshipful and artistic knowing. The process has four steps. It begins with the sitting still that makes it possible for us to *contemplate*. That contemplation prepares us to *perceive*. The perception then leads us to ask, "What might this mean?" which is the work of *interpretation*. When

František Kupka, *Madame Kupka among Verticals*

our interpretation is made, we are then ready to *respond*, through the myriad forms of justice, kindness, and going humbly with God that constitute the religious vocation. Here is a brief description of each of these steps.

1. Contemplation. In order to know what we see, we usually must take time to calm ourselves and to be at rest, although art can always arrest us and demand a response in the midst of busyness. Nevertheless, we are more likely to pay attention if we preface our moments of seeing and studying with rhythmic inhaling and exhaling, an act that many of us bring to meditation and prayer. As we are reminded in the introduction to the second volume of *Imaging the Word*, the ancient art of contemplation is one that encourages us to slow down, to read, and to take time to be open to God, to accounts from the Bible, as well as to associated images and poetic texts. Contemplation is a prerequisite for being open to God and for discovering and connecting the arts to both the Incarnate Word and to the circumstances of our lives.

2. Perception. The word "aesthetic" means "capable of being perceived by the senses." Perception is the moment in the act of seeing when we bring our eyes and ears and taste and touch to the encounter with any work of art. With students of the arts, it often helps to stimulate perception with a few leading questions, such as "What do you see?" (for example, an oil painting, a watercolor, a photograph, a woodcut, a sculpture), and to follow that with an opportunity for an overview of the work. This overview can be provoked by additional questions such as, What is the work about? What's its subject? What are five or ten or fifteen things you see in the work? These "things" might be objects or persons, but they might also be lines, colors, shapes, shadows, light, background, foreground. As these become subjects of our perception, the artwork before us comes alive, and we find ourselves educated and tutored beyond our initial impressions, so that we can move on to succeeding questions of perception and sensitivity. These might include: What does the work make you feel? Does anything in the work touch you? Are *you* anywhere in the work?

3. Interpretation. Once perception is engaged, we can then move on to the inevitable next question, "What do you think it means?" This is, of course, the question of interpretation, a wondrous step that has no right answer. We can make educated guesses, of course, but interpretation is actually more in the realm of religious reality than any other realm because it is about disclosure and revelation. The artist's intention often helps us to interpret, and we are wise to ask, "What did the artist intend here?" But it is also true that genuine works of art have a surplus of meaning. Viewers who encounter such works will discover that with second, third, and subsequent meetings, the works unveil facets of themselves that were not always apparent initially.

Jacob Lawrence, *Harriet Tubman and the
Promised Land*

4. Response. What, if anything, does a particular work of art ask from us? Does it impel us to *do* anything? Although not every work will touch us, and each of us will have particular favorites, it is nevertheless true that our response to a genuine work of art is often an act of gratitude or thanksgiving, a prayerful "thank you." We find our spirits moved by the arts. Not only our eyes and our minds, but our hearts and our emotions recognize that with the arts, we are in the presence of something holy. Sometimes art brings us to our knees; at other times it exalts us and impels us to dance or to play. Each of these is a form of worship, although other responses are part of worship too—the works of justice to which a photograph such as Margaret Bourke-White's *Louisville, Kentucky, Flood Victims* (page 52) might impel us; the work to ban handguns and assault weapons to save children from violence (page 90); the work of making music like Chapin's *Ruby Green Sings* (page 213); the work of telling stories in the manner of the storyteller to Harriet Tubman (page 39).

Testing the Process

We have already entered this process by our initial meeting with *The Red Staircase*. As a way of testing it further, look at Henry Tanner's *Annunciation* (page 93). Sit with it a while, without hurrying. Instead of analyzing it, let it address you, and allow its silence to envelop you. Be in its presence.

When you are ready, examine the painting carefully. What do you notice first? What words might you use to describe the figure sitting on the bed? Where is she looking? At whom, if anyone, is she looking? Examine her clothing and the bed clothing too. How would you describe these? What are some of the many colors that surround her? What shapes do you notice? Have you ever seen floor tiles and rugs like the ones in the room? If so, where?

Now look at the brilliant color at the left of the painting. What do you see in the color? What words would you use to describe the white column that is in its center?

When you have taken time for perceptive engagement with the work, move on to its possible meaning. Recall that Tanner calls this painting *The Annunciation* and the young woman who is seated on the bed is obviously intended to be Mary at the moment the angel Gabriel visits her (Luke 1:26–38). What do you think it means that the angel is painted as light? What kind of feeling does the color and the light evoke in you? Can you say why? What can you tell of Mary's response by the expression on her face? What does the posture of her body say to you? Why and how would you describe the clasping of her hands? And what might it mean that the light spills over onto the bed even as far as the pillow?

Henry O. Tanner, *The Annunciation*

What does the word "annunciation" say to you? Does this painting evoke any moments of annunciation in your own life? In the life of your family? In the life of your people? Does the memory of how you felt at such moments reveal anything further about Mary's response? Conversely, does Mary's response illuminate yours in any way?

Finally, can you identify directions for living to which this work might lead you? Are there any concrete responses to which it calls you? Listen to your heart and to what each of your senses suggests to you.

Discerning the presence of our God in the midst of our daily lives is not always easy. However, if we discipline ourselves through the artistic acts of contemplation, perception, interpretation, and response and use them in our regular meetings with the arts, the effects of that discipline will spill over into our lives. Eventually we shall realize that every place is a sacred place, that every moment is filled with the divine Presence, and that the world is forever charged with the grandeur of God.

Maria Harris

Playing and Praying: Tips for Engaging Children with Art

"Pretty to look at, but not to touch" may work well when you and your children enter a store filled with fragile treasures. One grab from a shelf or innocent bump of a breakable may cause a crash that will cost you plenty. But when children enter the treasures found in *Imaging the Word*, encourage them to be active viewers, to touch, play, pray, and imagine wholeheartedly. The following suggestions will help you as a parent, teacher, or friend to lead children into the arts. The results of such experiences will surprise you. Together, child and adult, you may deepen your relationship with one another, with the arts, with the world, and with God.

1. Use the artwork to tell the story of God from Scripture.

• *Jonah* by Albert Pinkham Ryder from "The Word to Jonah" for Epiphany 3 (page 125).

Work with your child to find elements of Jonah's story in the painting, then encourage your child to tell you the story of Jonah from the painting.

2. Encourage children to identify with or enter into the story that the picture is telling.

• *Hallelujah* by Osmond Watson from "You Are Witnesses" for Easter 3 (page 202).

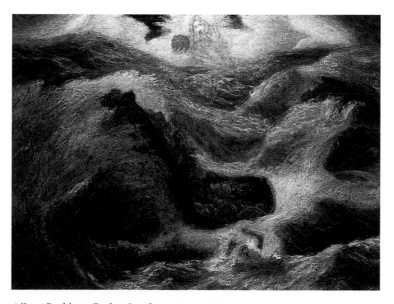

Albert Pinkham Ryder, *Jonah*

Church of Ixtepec, Oaxaca, Mexico,
Christ's Entry into Jerusalem

This relief sculpture shows the disciples sent by Jesus going forth filled with the spirit of joy, singing. Ask your children if they can imagine what these people are singing. What songs do people sing when they are very happy and excited to be doing something? What songs celebrate special occasions? Is there a special song that they would like to sing for Jesus? Sing it!

• *Christ's Entry into Jerusalem* from the Church of Ixtepec, Oaxaca, Mexico, from "Jerusalem" for Palm/Passion Sunday (page 180).

A *santos* is a folk woodcarving usually of saints. Here this *santos* is of Jesus and shows the mark of great love and care by the people of this parish. It is well painted, flowers surround it, and someone has even placed a slipper on Jesus' foot. Caring for the *santos* is one way of praying, of saying to Jesus that they love him and want to help him.

Encourage your children to draw a picture or make a *santos* of Jesus in the Palm Sunday procession or in another of their favorite stories about Jesus, such as the story of Jesus in the manger, or stories about Jesus healing or teaching people. Ask the children to include in their picture something that is special to them as a gift for Jesus, to help take care of him, to help him with his work, and to show him that they love him.

• *The Scream* by Edvard Munch and *Solstice* by Linda Post from "A New Teaching" for Epiphany 4 (pages 129, 131).

Compare with your child the feelings of the people in these paintings: Munch's scary, anguished, upset; Post's free, joyful, strong. Does your child recognize these very different feelings? Can she experiment with the different postures: cringing in fear, jumping for joy? Can she feel the difference in her own body?

Edvard Munch, *The Scream*, detail

Linda Post, *Solstice*, detail

Tell the story of Jesus from this passage, that he teaches with a new authority and can even cast out evil forces that cause people pain. Can she imagine what Jesus might have said to heal people and to bring them from fear to joy and freedom?

3. Encourage playfulness and surprise.

• *Beatitude* by Ben Shahn from "On the Sabbath?" for Proper 4 (page 231).

One of the themes of this entry is the paradox of Jesus' actions: a man of God who seems to be challenging one of God's most sacred laws, the Sabbath. Jesus surprised everyone! Can you encourage your child to remember other times when Jesus surprised his friends?

Ben Shahn, *Beatitude*

Ben Shahn also surprised his audience in the way he painted the wheat field. His painting gives the viewer the impression of seeing a field of golden wheat, but the wheat sheaves are in fact black! Can your child figure out how Shahn did this? Can your child create other pictures that surprise?

• *Altarpiece: Life of Christ* by Keith Haring from "God So Loved" for Lent 4 (page 173).

In this altarpiece, Keith Haring used his famous whimsical figures to show Jesus' love for all people. He used a metal loop to dig into wet plaster to make the characters. Then Haring covered his etching with gold and made it into a triptych (an altarpiece with three panels). What ways are the characters showing love? After looking at the characters, what might you pray about?

Encourage your child to use his imagination to create a Haring-type altarpiece for his room to show ways that God loves us. With bold colorful markers or crayons, have him draw characters and then fold the paper into three panels. Or, if possible, go outside and use colored-chalk to draw the figures on a sidewalk. Keith Haring also loved large public paintings.

4. Don't avoid the scary, the painful, or the sad. Create a safe and trusting environment for children to feel their feelings, ask their questions, and imagine realistic, hopeful alternatives.

• *Germany's Children Are Starving!* by Käthe Kollwitz from "Rain Down Bread" for Proper 20 (page 36).

This image may well be frightening to children, dealing as it does with apparently hungry children. Anticipate, even prompt some questions and feelings from your own

Käthe Kollowitz, *Germany's Children are Starving!*

children. Who are these children? What happened to them? Where are their parents? Could this happen to me? Why might God let this happen to them? How can God help them?

Kollwitz drew this for a German poster in 1924, a time of political and economic hardship. People begged on streets, knocked on doors, waited for soup and bread in huge municipal shelters. Help your children imagine a story about these children in which they receive promised "manna." How would this happen? If they planted a food garden and began to tend it? If people from around the world began to share? You may want to tell the children a story, perhaps the fable "Stone Soup" or "Nail Soup" where each person contributes a little and all are fed.

• *Boys with Kite* by Estelle Ishigo from "In One Body" for Proper 11 (page 259).

The theme of this unit has to do with reconciliation in Christ, breaking down the barriers that keep us from being "one body."

These little boys are taking the risk of being hurt on the barbed wire as they climb over it. Can your children imagine why they would take such a risk? You may want to tell your children the story of why these boys are behind barbed wire, the story of the internment of Japanese American families in camps during World War II.

Estelle Ishigo, *Boys with Kite*

You may want to talk about fences. What do they do? What good things, and what bad things? What kind of a fence is the one in the painting? What is it keeping these little boys from? Can your child imagine flying through the air on the tail of the kite, looking at the land beneath her? What kind of fences will she see? Will she see any kind of fences at all?

5. Use the artwork to connect your family's story with the story of God.

• *Presentation, Brazil* by Mev Puleo from "The Wise Ones" for Christmas 1 (page 105).

The old woman looks with delight upon this new baby. Perhaps she, like Anna in the Scripture story, sees a wonderful future for the community in the presence of this new life.

Can your child imagine what she might be thinking about or hoping for this child?

Use this picture as an opportunity to connect your child and your family's story with the story of Jesus. Tell again stories of your child's arrival—his birth or homecoming, baptism or dedication. How did his grandparents feel? What did his brothers and sisters say? What was the special joy and hope that your child created in your family and friends, as Jesus created for Simeon and Anna?

• *Seder Questions in Hebrew and English* from "Festival of Freedom" for Proper 18 (page 28).

Elie Wiesel comments that the Seder is conceived for children. It passes on their tradition to them and teaches them how to ask questions. Can you establish an occasional question/answer time with your child, encouraging her to wonder aloud about God, the world, the church? It is not necessary to produce all the answers, but to join her in thinking them through together, using your child's experiences as a way into insight about God.

6. Let the artwork connect the world's story with God's story.

• *Child with Gun* by Senad Gubelic from "Good News Coming" for Advent 3 (page 90).

Imagine what is happening all around the child and this soldier. Draw the scene around them. Where is the good news coming from? It looks like they are in a war zone. Is the war ending? Are people celebrating? What will happen to the soldier and the gun in peacetime? What will happen to the child?

Mev Puleo, *Presentation, Brazil*

מַה נִּשְׁתַּנָּה הַלַּיְלָה

הַזֶּה מִכָּל הַלֵּילוֹת.

Film still from *Footloose*

Salvador Dali, *Girl Standing
at the Window*

Mev Puleo, *Girls Praying*

7. Let the artwork suggest different ways to pray.

• Film still from *Footloose* from "Dance before God" for Proper 10 (page 256).

Tell your child the story of *Footloose* found in this entry. Talk about the story of David dancing for joy before God. Ask your child to make up a dance to tell God how happy she is. Does she, like David and the youth in *Footloose*, find that sometimes dancing is a better way to pray than sitting still and thinking about God?

• *Girl Standing at the Window* by Salvador Dali from "Keep Awake" for Advent 1 (page 83).

Does your child have a favorite window at which he daydreams? Ask him to draw a picture of it, and include what it is he looks for out the window—a friend coming to play, a parent coming home from work. Encourage him to draw what makes him feel good and hopeful when he looks out the window. Ask him if he ever talks to God through the window.

• *Girls Praying* by Mev Puleo from "Here I Am!" for Epiphany 2 (page 122).

These little girls are talking to God and listening for what God might have to say to them. Their heads are down, their eyes are closed, and their hands are folded. Does your child pray like this? Are there other ways that your child prays? Ask how your child talks to God, and where he or she listens for God's messages.

Susan A. Blain

19

Vassily Kandinsky, *Allerheiligen (All Saints')*

Pentec

The fruit of faithfulness grows daily into a

harvest of abundant life for the saints of God.   The season following the festival of Pentecost is the longest of the church year, stretching out over the six months from late spring to late autumn. Like a well-traveled old road that meanders through a beloved landscape, the season takes the church through many stories of the Hebrew Bible and the Christian Scriptures, inviting leisurely exploration of the themes that undergird our faith traditions. In the autumn during cycle A, the church lingers over the story of the Exodus, with its movements of call, of promise, of deliverance, and of law. The early days of the formation of the people of Israel are reflected upon in the light of the church's contemporary life. Where is the call to us today? Where is deliverance needed?

Toward the end of this long season comes the festival of All Saints', a celebration of the faith of the church throughout its history. Vassily Kandinsky's painting *Allerheiligen (All Saints')* captures the joy of the feast. We delight over the variety of calls and responses to God; we take courage from the examples of the saints for our own journeys of faith.

The color of the season following Pentecost is green, the color associated with life and growth. Green signals health and the presence of the invisible but powerful forces at work bringing earth to harvest. So with the fruit of faithfulness; it grows daily, unremarkably, into a harvest of abundant life for all the saints of God.

ost

Courage and delight in God's call

(Cycle A)

MOSES, MOSES!

Moses looked, and the bush was blazing, yet it was not
consumed. Then Moses said, "I must turn aside and look
at this great sight, and see why the bush is not burned up."
When God saw that Moses had turned aside to see,
God called to him out of the bush, "Moses, Moses!"

Exodus 3:2b–4a

Fire is the first and final
　　　　　mask of my God.

Nikos Kazantzakis

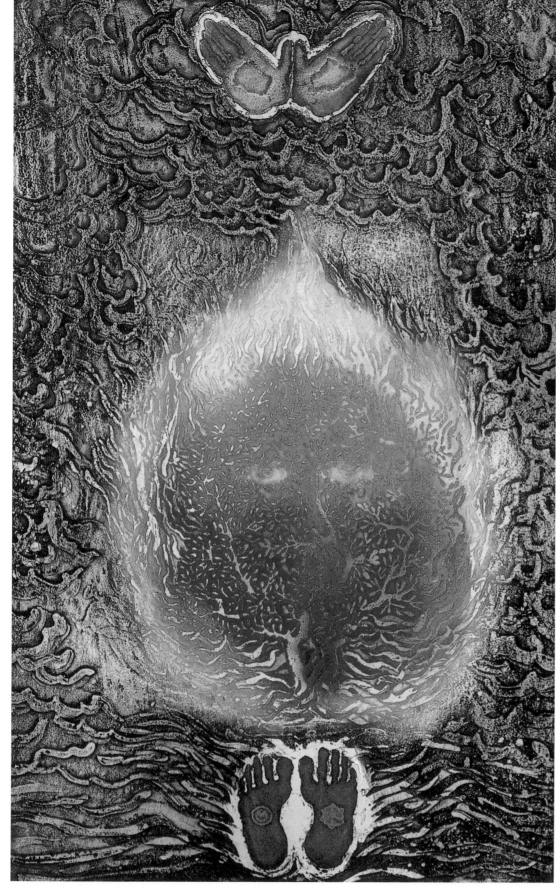

Inyan Wasicum Wakan—
the Holy White Stone Man—
that's what we call Moses.
He appeals to us. He goes up all
alone to the top of his mountain
like an Indian, to have his vision,
be all alone with his God,
who talks to him through fire,
bushes and rocks.

Lame Deer

You are a fire always
burning but never consuming;
you are a fire consuming
in your heat all the
soul's selfish love; you
are a fire lifting all
chill and giving light.
In your light you have
made me know your truth.
You are the light beyond
all light who gives the
mind's eye supernatural
light in such fullness
and perfection that you
bring clarity even to the light
of faith. In that faith I see
that my soul has life,
and in that light receives
you who are Light.

Catherine of Siena

Paul Koli, *The Burning Bush*

Symbols of the divinity are seen on the feet in this image.

Moses on Mount Sinai, from the *Psalter of Ingeburg of Denmark*

... God once spoke to people
　　by name.
The sun once imparted its flame.
One impulse persists as
　　our breath.
The other persists as our faith.

Robert Frost

In the first revelation to Moses, he is not sure what has happened; he has to be given some kind of sign. There's an immediate call to see a sign, the burning bush, just in order to come close, which is again the same thing; it's like knocking on the door, like feeling a hand on your shoulder. It's not in itself a message, but is a kind of awakening. Moses hears it. The Midrash says that later, Moses says to God, "Reveal yourself to me." And God says, "You cannot see my face. . . . I will cover you and you will see something anyway." And the Midrash says that God told Moses: "When I wanted it, you didn't want it. You hid your face. When you want it, I don't want it." Sometimes the only thing to be learned is this: when the call comes, jump!

Rabbi Adin Steinsaltz

In the fires of L.A. [spring 1992],
God is offering the community
of faith another burning bush
experience. In Exodus the burning
bush caught hold of Moses'
attention so that Moses could
hear God saying that it is the
world that sets God's agenda.
[Exodus 3] is very clear: I have
witnessed the misery of my
people; I have heard them crying
out because of their oppressors;
I know what they are suffering;
and I have come to rescue them
out of the hands of the Egyptians,
to bring them out of that country
and into a new land that flows
with milk and honey.

The fires of L.A. are the fires
of frustration and pain and misery
and oppression. They are an
indication of the frustration of
millions of people who cut across
the lines of class and color,
if we want to hear it . . . we must
listen to the burning bush.
To do otherwise would be to
squander God's grace.

James Lawson

Thuma Mina
Send Me Now

South African traditional song

And remember how final a hush
Then descended of old on the bush.

Robert Frost

This day shall be a day of remembrance for you.

You shall celebrate it as a festival to God;

throughout your generations you shall observe

it as a perpetual ordinance.

Exodus 12:14

remember

In every generation,
each man
is obliged to see himself
as though
he went out of Egypt.

In every generation,
every woman
is obliged to see herself
as though she went out
   from Egypt. . . .

E. M. Broner and Naomi Nimrod

Ken Heyman, *Nigerian Railsplitter*

מַה נִּשְׁתַּנָּה הַלַּיְלָה הַזֶּה מִכָּל הַלֵּילוֹת.

Passover Seder Meal in Jewish Tradition

Toward the beginning of the Seder meal each year, the youngest of the children present at the table asks the Four Questions:

How does this night differ from all other nights? On all other nights we eat either leavened or unleavened bread. Why on this night do we eat only unleavened bread?

On all other nights we eat all kinds of herbs. Why on this night do we eat only bitter herbs?

On all other nights we need not dip our herbs even once. Why on this night do we need to dip twice?

On all other nights we eat either sitting or reclining. Why on this night must we all recline?

These questions are simple and practical. . . . The entire Seder has been conceived for children. We must teach them how to ask questions. And therefore, for guidance, we offer them the proverbial Four Questions. Then, it is up to each child to ask his [or her] own.

A Passover Haggadah as Commented upon by Elie Wiesel

A memory from my town, Sighet: Our Seder table was never without a stranger. I remember that we went from one synagogue to the other, from one house of study to the other, looking for a stranger without whom our holiday would be incomplete. And this was true of most Jews in my town and probably of most Jews in other towns. On Passover eve, the poor, the uprooted, the unhappy were the most sought after, the most beloved guests. It was for them and with them that we recited: "This year we are still slaves. Next year may we all be free." Without comforting our impoverished guest, our riches would shame us. And so we were grateful to him. In some towns, before Passover, Jews would raise funds discreetly: One by one, they would enter a room in the community house. There they would find a dish filled with money. Those who had money left some; those who needed money took some. No one knew how much was given or how much was taken. Thus, the needy were cared for with dignity.

Elie Wiesel

Let them praise God's name with dancing,

    making melody to God with tambourine and lyre.

Psalm 149:3

Meichel Pressman, *The Seder*

Adir Hu
God of Might

1 A - dir hu,   a - dir hu,   yiv-
1 God of might,   God of right,
2 We en - slaved   thus were saved

neh vei - to b' - ka - rov,   bim - hei - ra
we would bow be - fore you,   sing your praise
through God's might ap - pear - ing,   so we pray

bim - hei - ra b' - ya - mei - nu, b' - ka - rov Eil b' - nei,
in these days, cel - e - brate your glo - ry, as we hear
for the day when we shall be hear - ing free - dom's call

eil b' - nei,   b'nei veit - cha b' - ka - rov.
year by year,   free - dom's won - drous sto - ry.
reach - ing all,   the peo - ple's God re - ver - ing.

From Howard I. Bogot and Robert J. Orkand, *A Children's Haggadah* (New York: Central Conference of American Rabbis, 1994), 70. Used by permission.

THROUGH THE SEA

Then Moses stretched out his hand over the sea. God drove the sea back by a strong east wind all night, and turned the sea into dry land; the waters were divided. The Israelites went into the sea on dry ground, the waters forming a wall for them on their right and on their left.

Exodus 14:21–22

Shalom of Safed, *The Exodus with the Pillar of Fire*

Why is it, O sea, that you flee?
  O Jordan, that you turn back?
O mountains, that you skip like rams?
  O hills, like lambs?

Tremble, O earth, at the presence of God,
  at the presence of the God of Jacob,
who turns the rock into a pool of water,
  the flint into a spring of water.

Psalm 114:5–8

And in That Drowning Instant

And in that drowning instant as
the water heightened over me
it suddenly did come to pass
my preterite eternity
the image of myself intent
on several freedoms
    fading to

myself in yellowed basel-print
vanishing

    into ghetto Jew
a face among the face of
the rapt disciples hearkening
the raptures of the Baalshem Tov
explaining Torah

    vanishing
amidst the water's flickering green
to show me in old Amsterdam
which topples

    into a new scene
Cordova where an Abraham
faces inquisitors

    the face
is suddenly beneath the arch
whose Latin script the waves erase
and flashes now the backward march
of many
    I among them
        to
Jerusalem-gate and Temple-door!

For the third time my body rises
and finds the good, the lasting shore!

A. M. Klein

The poet's identity merges with the identity of the Jewish people as he experiences a vision of himself as a participant in different ages of Jewish history, struggling for freedom and enduring from the beginning into an eternity rooted in the past.

The women wept and I wept. I too cried for the lost people, their ancestors and mine. But I was also weeping with a curious joy. Despite the murders, rapes and suicides, we had survived. The middle passage and the auction block had not erased us. Not humiliations nor lynchings, individual cruelties nor collective oppression had been able to eradicate us from the earth. We had come through despite our own ignorance and gullibility, and the ignorance and rapacious greed of our assailants.

There was much to cry for, much to mourn, but in my heart I felt exalted knowing there was much to celebrate. Although separated from our language, our families and customs, we had dared to continue to live. We had crossed the unknowable oceans in chains and had written its mystery into "Deep River, my home is over Jordan." Through the centuries of despair and dislocation, we had been creative, because we faced down death by daring to hope.

Maya Angelou

Crashing Waters at Creation

Crashing Waters at creation
    ordered by the spirit's breath,
First to witness day's beginning
    from the brightness of night's death.

Parting water stood and trembled,
    as the captives passed on through,
Washing off the chains of bondage—
    channel to a life made new.

Cleansing water once at Jordan
    closed around the One foretold,
Opened to reveal the glory
    ever new and ever old.

Living water, never ending,
    quench the thirst and flood the soul.
Wellspring, source of life eternal,
    drench our dryness, make us whole.

Sylvia G. Dunstan

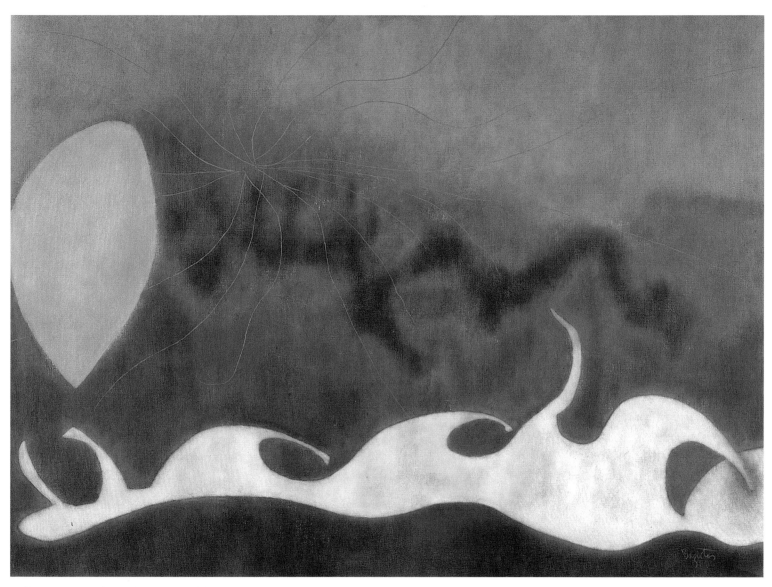

William Baziotes, *The Beach*

The movement and power of the sea is imaged in Baziotes's *The Beach*, which captures the moment before plunging into the surf.

Aaron: We are cut free from Pharaoh's hand. We march to the Promised Land.

Ben: It's Canaan or bust!

Rachel: Goodnight, Pharaoh. Sleep well. It's going to be a long night.

Aaron: Shout it one last time for *all* of Egypt to hear. Who has freedom?

Slaves: We have freedom! We have freedom!

Miriam: Praise the Lord!

Slaves: The Lord's name be praised.

Moses: We're on our way!

Hal Hopson, *Moses and the Freedom Fanatics*

R A I N   D O W N   B R E A D

Ercole de Roberti, *The Israelites Gathering Manna*

The whole congregation of the Israelites

complained against Moses and Aaron

in the wilderness. Then God said to Moses,

"I am going to rain bread from heaven for

you, and each day the people shall go out

and gather enough for that day. In that way

I will test them, whether they will follow

my instruction or not."

Exodus 16:2, 4

Psalm 149

We are lost in the wilderness, O God;
    we thirst and hunger for thee.
Our lips are parched with silence;
    our souls dried up.

In the desert of hopelessness we tread
    through the hot sands of human degradation.
Wandering on the still lethargic prairies of apathy,
    thy people are lost.

Through the sins of our existence
    we have become alienated from thee.
Yet it has been through our earthly oppression
    that we have found thee in closeness.

Deliver thy people, O God;
    save us from destruction.
For it is by our faith that we shall be rescued;
    and we shall freely drink from thine oasis of love.

Benjamin Chavis, Jr.

In my dreams, I walk among the ruins
of the old part of town
looking for a bit of stale bread.

My mother and I inhale the fumes of gunpowder.
I imagine it to be the smell of pies, cakes, and kebab.

A shot rings out from a nearby hill. We hurry.
Though it's only nine o'clock, we might by hurrying
toward a grenade marked "ours."

An explosion rings out in the street of dignity.
Many people are wounded—
sisters, brothers, mothers, fathers.

I reach out to touch a trembling, injured hand.
I touch death itself.

Terrified, I realize this is not a dream.
It is just another day in Sarajevo.

Edina, 12, from Sarajevo

Käthe Kollwitz, *Germany's Children Are Starving!*

stranger to our table

Manna from Heaven, Great Malvern Priory, Worcester, Great Britain

Moses dwelt in the desert with those around him. He grew vigilant, watching a movement by which he deserted himself. Many not as active as he languished without their former comforts and hiding places. They could not leave. When they were hungry, manna fell from heaven, and they were fed; but a disquiet robbed them of a vision of the miracle. There was only deprivation and their unforsaken greed. They lived for a promise and a dream, oblivious to the holy place of their passage.

David Applebaum

Film still from *Edward Scissorhands*

Snow-like ice, rather than manna, falls from the heavens as the young woman remembers her love for Edward Scissorhands. Grace falls from above.

As bread that was scattered on the hillside,
was gathered together and made one,
so too, we, your people,
scattered throughout the world,
are gathered together around your table
and become one.

As grapes grown in the field
are gathered together and pressed into wine,
so too are we drawn together
and pressed by our times to share a common lot
and are transformed into your life-blood
for all.

So let us prepare to eat and drink
as Jesus taught us:
inviting the stranger to our table
and welcoming the poor.
May their absence serve to remind us
of the divisions this Eucharist seeks to heal.
And may their presence help transform us
into the Body of Christ we share.

Adapted from *The Didache*

TELL THE GLORIOUS DEEDS

We will not hide them from their children;

we will tell to the coming generation

the glorious deeds of God, and God's might,

and the wonders that God has done.

Psalm 78:4

I can only explain
my own life
and the events of the
times in which
I've lived in the context
of faith—a biblical
faith that continues
to see the hand
of God working in
the affairs of the
children of creation.

This is a simple
proclamation of my
understanding of life.
My life has unfolded
around me in
ways that fill me
with awe and wonder.
The testimony
of men and women
down through the
ages can help us to
discover or discern
a spiritual direction
for our lives.

Andrew Young

Jacob Lawrence, *Harriet Tubman and the Promised Land*

Underneath the stars, the slave girl
Harriet Tubman heard the story of Moses
and the Hebrews' march to freedom.
She lived the story as an adult leading slaves
to freedom through the Underground Railroad.

Harriet, hear tell
About the Promised Land,
How Moses led the slaves
Over Egypt's sand.

How Pharaoh's heart
Was hard as stone.
How the Lord told Moses
He was not alone.

Jacob Lawrence

Once upon a time…

In the beginning, when God was creating the heavens and the earth…

Ainslie Roberts, *The Storyteller*

Memory, imagination, and the human capacity to embody drama are the tools employed by this storyteller of the indigenous people of Australia to offer to his young audience both their history and a vision for their future. Between that history and that vision their story communicates what it is for them to be human.

Moyers:

Myths are stories of our search through the ages for the truth, for meaning, for significance. We need to tell our story and to understand our story. We all need to understand death and to cope with death, and we all need help in our passages from birth to life and then to death. We need for life to signify, to touch the eternal, to understand the mysterious, to find out who we are.

Campbell:

People say that what we're all seeking is meaning for life. I don't think that's what we're really seeking. I think what we're seeking is an experience of being alive, so that our life experience on the purely physical plane will have resonance within our own innermost being and reality, so that we actually feel the rapture of being alive.

Dialogue between Joseph Campbell and Bill Moyers, *The Power of Myth*

Story Screen at St. Mark's Episcopal Church, New Canaan, Connecticut

The congregation who views the screen recalls the stories of the Bible through symbols.

Our faith draws us together this day.
Let us trust enough to open our ears
and our hearts.

**We have heard of God's miracles in other
times; our ancestors have kept the story
alive for us.**

Give ear, all people, to God's word for today.
Taste the bounty of God's blessing here
and now.

**We long for a faith that makes sense today.
We want to keep the story alive for new
generations.**

God's revelation is for all people, near
and far. God is waiting to communicate
with you and me.

**May God have mercy on us and all people.
Surely God's will shall be made known
to us.**

Lavon Bayler

…And they lived happily ever after.
…"Behold, I make
all things new."

YOU SHALL . . .

I am the Sovereign your God, who brought you

out of the land of Egypt, out of the house of slavery;

you shall have no other gods before me.

Exodus 20:2–3

Isn't that what religion is all about? I think so—to tell you how to behave. God made a Covenant with our people, that's what we learned the other day in Hebrew School. Moses was given the Ten Commandments, and that's the biggest time in our history, when that happened. Just because we can't get all A's, make a perfect record, doesn't mean we shouldn't keep trying.

Tony, age 11

Grade 4 at St. Francis
Xavier School,
Moses Quilt

This quilt was created
by the students in fourth
grade at St. Francis Xavier
School in Gettysburg,
Pennsylvania. As a way
of learning the stories
about Moses, students
designed all the images
and then cut pieces
from various fabrics to
make this large quilt.
After hanging in the local
church for a few months
it was sent to a church
community in Kenya.

Tadao Tanaka, *The Ten Commandments*

*Let me say it
as radically
and provocatively
as possible.
We cannot be
Christians without
first being Jews,
or more accurately,
without knowing
the method of the Jew.*

*We cannot
understand the
meaning of forgiveness
unless we first
throw ourselves into
a radical concern
about the nature
of right moral action.*

*We cannot be
delivered from the
curse of the law
unless first of all
we know, contemplate,
and strive to
keep the law.*

*We cannot comprehend
acceptance and grace
unless we have
first felt the intensity
of the Jewish experience
of God's command
to fulfill the law.*

Don Browning

God's universe is perfect,
    awing the mind.
God's truth is subtle,
    baffling the intellect.
God's law is complete,
    quickening the breath.
God's compassion is fathomless,
    refreshing the soul.
God's justice is absolute,
    lighting up the eyes.
God's love is radiant,
    rejoicing the heart,
more precious than the finest gold,
    sweeter than honey from the comb.

Psalm 19, as translated by Stephen Mitchell

Be joyful

Be joyful in my commandment.

John Updike

The purpose of the laws of the Torah is to promote compassion, loving-kindness and peace in the world.

Moses Maimonides

Hear the commandments of God:
I am the Holy One, your God,
who brought you out of bondage.
You shall have no other gods but me.
God, have mercy on us
and guide us in your way.
You shall not make for yourself any idol.
God, have mercy on us
and guide us in your way.
You shall not invoke with malice
the name of the Holy One, your God.
God, have mercy on us
and guide us in your way.
Remember the Sabbath day and keep it holy.
God, have mercy on us
and guide us in your way.
Honor your father and your mother.
God, have mercy on us
and guide us in your way.
You shall not commit murder.

God, have mercy on us
and guide us in your way.
You shall not commit adultery.
God, have mercy on us
and guide us in your way.
You shall not steal.
God, have mercy on us
and guide us in your way.
You shall not be a false witness.
God, have mercy on us
and guide us in your way.
You shall not covet anything
that belongs to your neighbor.
God, have mercy on us
and guide us in your way.
Jesus said the first commandment is:
The Holy One, our God, is the only Holy One;
and you shall love the Holy One, your God,
with all your heart, and with all your soul,
and with all your mind,
and with all your strength.
The second commandment is this:
You shall love your neighbor
as you love yourself.
No other commandment is greater than these.

Exodus 20:1–17 and Mark 12:29–31, adapted
from the *Book of Worship, United Church of Christ*

Sorel Etrog, *Moses*

This sculpture manages to convey both the weight of the commandments (given in stone, the medium of the piece) and the joy of the Law, as the base of the sculpture seems almost to dance as it balances on its pedestal.

MANY CALLED, FEW CHOSEN

Jesus said, "The dominion of heaven may be compared to a king who gave a wedding banquet for his son. He sent his slaves to call those who had been invited to the wedding banquet, but they would not come. For many are called but few are chosen."

Matthew 22:2–3, 14

You that do truly and earnestly repent you of your sins to Almighty God, and be in love and charity with your neighbors, and intend to lead a new life, following the commandments to God, and walking from henceforth in his holy ways; Draw near, and take this holy sacrament to your comfort; make your humble confession to Almighty God, and to his holy church here gathered together in his name, meekly kneeling upon your knees.

"Invitation to Communion" from *The Book of Common Prayer*, 1549

Rembrandt Harmensz van Rijn, *The Parable of the Unworthy Wedding Guest*

[God's] invitation is most gracious; all are invited, both bad and good.

But just because all are invited does not mean there are no standards, no expectations of the guests.

A wedding garment (kingdom talk for new life, righteous conduct) is expected.

Fred Craddock

Diego Rivera, *Dance in Tehuantepec*

put on Christ
and become a new creation

When the ruler came in to see the company
at the table, he observed one person who was not
dressed for a wedding. "My friend," said the
ruler, "how do you come to be here without your
wedding clothes?" He had nothing to say.
The ruler then said to his attendants, "Bind him
hand and foot; and turn him out into the night."

Matthew 22:11–13

We know all are invited, but not all may stay!
Only those who let themselves be transformed here
   those willing to become new people
   to "put on Christ"
   and become a "new creation"
in the unimaginable patterns of the God of life—

. . .

Textured with struggle and joy,
colored with passion and compassion,
laced with faith, hope and love—

Wedding guests in living garments
fully engaged in God's feast of life.

Susan A. Blain

Change

Wait for me, Lord: I'm coming!
Wait for me, Lord: I'm getting dressed!

I am clothing my eyes with goodness
to look at everyone in friendship.

I am clothing my hands with peace
to forgive without keeping track.

I am clothing my lips with a smile
to offer joy all day long.

I am clothing my body and my heart
with prayer
to turn towards you,
Lord whom I love.

Now I am ready!
It's me! Do you recognize me?
I have put on my best clothing!

Charles Singer

Jesus said, "Show me the coin used for the tax." And they brought him a denarius. Then Jesus said to them, "Whose head is this, and whose title?" They answered, "The emperor's." Then Jesus said to them, "Give therefore to the emperor the things that are the emperor's, and to God the things that are God's." When they heard this, they were amazed.

Matthew 22:19–22a

For humanity was made to God's image and likeness. . . . Our true and lasting good therefore is to be stamped anew by regeneration. This seems to me the sense which wise interpreters have applied to our Lord's words upon looking at Caesar's tribute money: *Render to Caesar the things that are Caesar's, and to God the things that are God's.* It is as if Jesus had said: God, like Caesar, demands from us the impression of God's own image. Just as we repay Caesar's coinage to Caesar, so return the soul to God, shining and stamped with the light of God's countenance.

St. Augustine

Titian, *The Tribute Money*

Margaret Bourke-White, *Flood Victims, Louisville, Kentucky*

The photographer exploits the irony implicit in the contrast between the billboard's proclamation of a society's ideal—white, prosperous, and seemingly protected by economic privilege from the elements—and the reality of the human beings who gather under it—black, poor, vulnerable.

"There are three great things that happen to a man in his lifetime.

Buying a house . . . a car . . . and a new color TV.
That is what America is all about."

Archie Bunker in the television series *All in the Family*

Archie Bunker, the main character on the popular television series *All in the Family*, was portrayed in stereotypical terms as one who embodied all the uncritical assumptions of American life, with its racism, sexism, and materialism.

[God] coined us
in [God's] image. . . .
We are [God's] money,
and we should be spent. . . .
Money should circulate,
we should circulate;
money should go from hand to hand,
we should go from hand to hand; . . .
money should be used,
we should be used; . . .
money is going to be worn,
we should be going to be worn.

We should be spent,
we are coins,
God is trying to use us,
to pay off our debts,
to pay off the debts we owe each other
here on earth. . . .

Let us risk being used,
and we will be increased,
and the end will be glory. . . .

Joseph Donders

Stamp me in your heart,
Upon your limbs,
Sear my emblem deep
Into your skin.

For love is as strong as death,
Harsh as the grave.
Its tongues are flames, a fierce
And holy blaze.

Endless seas and floods,
Torrents and rivers
Never put out love's
Infinite fires.

Marcia Falk

God, you have been our dwelling place in all generations. Before the mountains were brought forth, or ever you had formed the earth and the world, from everlasting to everlasting you are God.

Psalm 90:1–2

We have all had at least fleetingly, an experience of home. Home is where no one ever forgets your name. Home is where no matter what you have done, you will be confronted, forgiven, and accepted. Home is where there is always a place for you at the table. . . . The heart of justice is participation in God's economy or God's household.

Douglas Meeks

Arthur B. Davies, *Hosannah of the Mountains*

Throughout the early 1900s, Davies' pastoral scenes took on a mystical quality by use of space, light, and rich color. In *Hosannah of the Mountains* the contrasts between tree and child are enormous. Although dwarfed by the mammoth trees, the children play protected in the space.

. . . Tonight I will sleep beneath your feet, O Lord of the mountains and valleys, ruler of the trees and vines. I will rest in your love, with you protecting me as a father protects his children, with you watching over me as a mother watches over her children. Then tomorrow the sun will rise and I will not know where I am; but I know that you will guide my footsteps.

A Sioux prayer

When we are made aware that all around us changes, and that those we cherish must pass away, the human spirit yearns for the constant and the lasting. Then more than ever we need to find a relation to something reliable and enduring as a refuge from all that is not.

James Luther Mays

Charles Burchfield, *Six O'Clock*

The ache for home lives in all of us, the safe place where we can go as we are and not be questioned. It impels mighty ambitions and dangerous capers. We amass great fortunes at the cost of our souls, or risk our lives in drug dens from London's Soho, to San Francisco's Haight-Ashbury. We shout in Baptist churches, wear yarmulkes and wigs and argue even the tiniest points in the Torah, or worship the sun and refuse to kill cows for the starving. Hoping that by doing these things, home will find us acceptable or failing that, that we will forget our awful yearning for it.

Maya Angelou

Pax

All that matters is to be at one with the living God
to be a creature in the house of the God of Life.

Like a cat asleep on a chair
at peace, in peace
and at one with the master of the house, with the mistress,
at home, at home in the house of the living,
sleeping on the hearth, and yawning before the fire.

Sleeping on the hearth of the living world
yawning at home before the fire of life
feeling the presence of the living God
like a great reassurance
a deep calm in the heart
a presence
as of the master sitting at the board
in his own and greater being,
in the house of life.

D. H. Lawrence

Rembrandt Harmensz van Rijn, *Holy Family with Cat and Snake*, detail

**You awake us to delight
in your praises;
for you made us for yourself,
and our hearts
are restless until they
rest in You.**

St. Augustine

I will bring you home;
I love you and you are mine.

David Haas

Some wandered in desert wastes, finding no way to an inhabited town;

hungry and thirsty, their soul fainted within them. Then they cried to God

in their trouble, and God delivered them from their distress. And there

God lets the hungry live, and they establish a town to live in.

Psalm 107:4–6, 36

In all these ways the psalm teaches the congregation and its members to understand themselves as the redeemed. Most of all and first of all they are the sinners and the helpless whose cry to God has been answered by [God's] hesed. We are the hungry and thirsty who have been fed. We are the bound who have been liberated. We are the sinners deserving death who have been given life. We are the fearful before the terrors of existence who have been given hope.

James Mays

Andrew Wyeth, *Christina's World*

The figure of the woman twisting toward the quiet farmhouse suggests the yearning for and struggle to achieve community.

Up-Hill

Does the road wind up-hill all the way?
    Yes, to the very end.
Will the day's journey take the whole long day?
    From morn to night, my friend.

But is there for the night a resting-place?
    A roof for when the slow dark hours begin.
May not the darkness hide it from my face?
    You cannot miss that inn.

Shall I meet other wayfarers at night?
    Those who have gone before.
Then must I knock, or call when just in sight?
    They will not keep you standing at that door.

Shall I find comfort, travel-sore and weak?
    Of labour you shall find the sum.
Will there be beds for me and all who seek?
    Yea, beds for all who come.

Christina Rossetti

Andrew Wyeth, *Christina's World*, detail

One night, while I was cooking supper, I suddenly got very lonely and felt burdened down. I stopped cooking, got my Bible, and sat down to read. Shortly after I started I lost sight of the world and saw myself (in the spirit) being led down a dark and lonely road, and as I went down the road it seemed to close behind me. I was praying inwardly to God saying, "Lord, have mercy!" For some reason I was caused to look up, and I saw a light on my right. I said, "Lord, where am I?" He answered, "The road you are on leads to hell, but the road on your right leads to heaven."

I looked down that dark pathway and saw what he called "the gulf of despair." I looked again and saw, as it were, human souls piled like timber, and everything was gloom and sadness. I cried to the Lord to deliver my soul, and he lifted me from that gulf of darkness and started me to traveling on the upward road.

Anonymous, from *God Struck Me Dead: Voices of Ex-Slaves*

Lord,

help us find the well
where you await us
at every stage of our lives.
And we shall set out again,
thirsting, at last,
for none but the living water
which you have promised us.

Pierre Talec

Anonymous,
Depiction of a Medieval Town

The unknown medieval artist
offers a picture of idyllic community
collaboration.

There is a river whose streams make glad the city of God,
the holy habitation of the Most High.
God is in the midst of the city; it shall not be moved.

Psalm 46:4-5a

THEIR DEEDS FOLLOW

And I heard a voice from heaven saying, "Write this: Blessed are the dead who from now on die in God." "Yes," says the Spirit, "they will rest from their labors, and their deeds follow them."

Revelation 14:13

When great souls die,
the air around us becomes
light, rare, sterile.
We breathe, briefly.
Our eyes, briefly,
see with
a hurtful clarity.
Our memory, suddenly sharpened,
examines,
gnaws on kind words
unsaid, promised walks never taken. . . .

And when great souls die,
after a period peace blooms,
slowly and always
irregularly. Spaces fill
with a kind of
soothing electric vibration.
Our senses, restored, never
to be the same, whisper to us.
They existed.
We can be. Be and be
better. For they existed.

Maya Angelou, from "Ailey, Baldwin, Floyd,
Killens and Mayfield"

Gerárd Valcin, *Visit to the Departed*

Be Merry, really Merry.

The life
of a Christian
should be
a perpetual jubilee,
a prelude
to the festivals
of eternity.

Theophane Venard

Wassily Kandinsky, *Allerheiligen (All Saints')*

The Last Day is portrayed as joyful confusion
in response to the trumpet's call.

The Saints Are Standing Row on Row

The saints are standing row on row
engulfed in light and peace,
stand face to face with God their King
whose love will never cease.

King David sings with harp and lyre
he's cantor of the town,
and Mary sings Magnificat
before her lowborn son.

Now Simeon begins his song
with tambourine and drum
while Miriam and Hannah sing
ta-rum, ta-rum, ta-rum.

And Luther sings just like a swan,
while John Sebastian Bach,
the great, great Bach directs the choir. . . .

There's Louis Armstrong with his horn
and Israel with its psalms.
The pious take their usual place
and gravely wave their palms.

From every nation they have come
to sing in this great choir,
their music raises up to God
whose face is like a fire.

Author unknown, translated from the
Dutch by Gracia Grindal

CHOOSE THIS DAY

Joshua said, "Now if you are unwilling to serve God,

choose this day whom you will serve, whether the gods

your ancestors served in the region beyond the River

or the gods of the Amorites in whose land you are living;

but as for me and my household, we will serve God."

Joshua 24:15

For Israel, the moment at Shechem was decisive. Behind them was God's promise made good. Now they were a nation in a promised land. Ahead of them, a question. Would they be faithful to the God who had been faithful to them?

Synthia Saint James, *Visions*

The image of Shechem is suggested by these figures all turning toward the sun, for it was at Shechem that the nation of Israel was configured for the first time as members of all twelve tribes met and agreed to serve God.

Gotta Serve Somebody

You may be an ambassador to England or France,
You may like to gamble, you might like to dance.
You may be the heavyweight champion of the world,
You might be a socialite with a long string of pearls.

But you're gonna have to serve somebody, yes indeed,
You're gonna have to serve somebody.
Well it may be the devil, or it may be the Lord,
But you're gonna have to serve somebody. . . .

Might like to wear cotton, you might like to wear silk.
Might like to drink whiskey, might like to drink milk.
You might like to eat caviar, you might like to eat bread.
You might be sleeping on the floor, sleeping in a king-sized bed.

But you're gonna have to serve somebody, yes indeed,
You're gonna have to serve somebody.
Well it may be the devil, or it may be the Lord,
But you're gonna have to serve somebody. . . .

Bob Dylan

One day Leonie [an older sister], no doubt thinking she was too old to play with dolls, came to us both with a basket filled with their clothes, ribbons, and other odds and ends. Her own doll was on top. She said, "Here you are, darlings. Take what you want." Celine took a little bundle of silk braid. I thought for a moment, then stretched out my hand and declared: "I choose everything," and, without more ado, I carried off the lot. Everyone thought this quite fair.

This episode sums up the whole of my life. . . . My God, I choose all. I do not want to be a saint by halves.

Therese Martin, a nineteenth-century mystic living in France

Choose, choose, choose
to fight or run
to sleep or read
to study or play
to be faithful or promiscuous
to obey or rebel
to yield or resist
to create or destroy
to repent or deny
to forgive or resent
to save or spend
to take risks or be cautious
to dream
to trust
Who will I trust? Who will I serve? Who will I please?
The crowd, the fashion, the neighbors?
For what will I sacrifice . . . ?
Choose this day. . . .

Paulo Solari

Sandra Jorgensen, *Roads*

Not only nations, but also individuals, are confronted with the choice whether to serve God.

choose

choose

The Road Not Taken

Two roads diverged in a wood,
And sorry I could not travel both
And be one traveler, long I stood
And looked down one as far as I could
To where it bent in the undergrowth;

Then took the other, just as fair,
And having perhaps the better claim
Because it was grassy and wanted wear;
Though as for that, the passing there
Had worn them really about the same,
And both that morning equally lay
In leaves no step had trodden black.
Oh, I kept the first for another day!
Yet knowing how way leads on to way,
I doubted if I should ever come back.

I shall be telling this with a sigh
Somewhere ages and ages hence:
Two roads diverged in a wood, and I—
I took the one less traveled by,
and that has made all the difference.

Robert Frost

O Lord our God,

we thank you for the many people throughout the ages

who have followed your way of life joyfully:

for the many saints and martyrs, men and women,

who have offered up their very lives,

so that your life abundant may become manifest.

For your love and faithfulness we will at all times praise you.

O Lord, we thank you for those who chose the way of Jesus Christ.

In the midst of trial, they held out hope,

in the midst of hatred, they kindled love;

in the midst of persecutions, they witnessed to your power;

in the midst of despair, they clung to your promise.

For your love and faithfulness we will at all times praise you.

O Lord, we thank you for the truth they passed on to us:

that it is by giving that we receive;

it is by becoming weak that we shall be strong;

it is by loving others that we shall be loved;

it is by offering ourselves that your kingdom shall unfold;

it is by dying that we shall inherit life everlasting.

Lord, give us courage to follow your way of life.

For your love and faithfulness we will at all times praise you.

National Council of Churches of the Philippines

ACCORDING TO ABILITY

Jesus said, "For it is as if someone, going on a journey, summoned slaves and entrusted property to them; giving to one five talents, to another two, to another one, all according to their ability; and went away. After a long time the master of those slaves came and settled accounts with them.

Matthew 25:14–15, 19

[Take account of] the high risk activity of the first two servants. They doubled the money entrusted to them, hardly a possibility without running the risk of losing the original investment. . . . The major themes of the Christian faith—caring, giving, witnessing, trusting, loving, hoping—cannot be understood or lived without risk.

Fred Craddock

The Wind, One Brilliant Day

The wind, one brilliant day, called
to my soul with an odor of jasmine

"In return for the odor of my jasmine,
I'd like all the odor of your roses."
"I have no roses; all the flowers
in my garden are dead."

"Well then, I'll take the withered petals
and the yellow leaves and the waters
    of the fountain."

The wind left, And I wept. And I said
    to myself:
"What have you done with the garden
    that was entrusted
to you?"

Antonio Machado

Glen Strock, *Parable of the Talents*

71

"If I were the Creator," Nathan said, "most of all, I'd want my creatures to live every minute of their life, not be so afraid of doing something wrong that they failed to savor the feast I'd prepared for them. I'd want my people to plant, and swim, and taste and see, and play. As the sunsets' and the rainbows' creator, I'd love these purple and acid-greens you've painted this room, and I would be glad you risked loving."

Grant Spradling

Glen Strock,
Parable of the Talents, detail

Our Deepest Fear

Our deepest fear is not that we are inadequate.
Our deepest fear is that we are powerful beyond measure.
It is our light, not our darkness, that most frightens us.
We ask ourselves, who am I to be brilliant, gorgeous,
    talented and fabulous?
Actually, who are you *not* to be?
You are a child of God.
Your playing small doesn't serve the world.
There's nothing enlightened about shrinking so that
    other people won't feel insecure around you.
We were born to make manifest the glory of God
    that is within us.
It's not just in some of us, it's in everyone.
And as we let our light shine,
we unconsciously give other people permission
    to do the same.
As we are liberated from our own fear,
our presence automatically liberates others.

Nelson Mandela, 1994 Inaugural Speech

Harlem

What happens to a dream deferred?
Does it dry up
like a raisin in the sun?

Or fester like a sore—
and then run?
Does it stink like rotten meat?
Or crust and sugar over—
like a syrupy sweet?

Maybe it sags

like a heavy load.

or does it explode?

Langston Hughes

O God, you claim me as your partner, respecting me,
trusting me,
tussling with me.
Support me
as I dare to be vulnerable with you,
encourage me as I dare to take risks with you,
and together we can transform our world.

Brigid Rees

Carmen Lomas Garza, *Ofrendo para Antonio Lomas (Offering to Antonio Lomas)*

In this large-scale altar, the artist depicts an offering honoring and celebrating all aspects of the life of her grandfather, Antonio Lomas.

THE LEAST OF THESE

T ruly I tell you, just as

you did it to one of the

least of these who are

members of my family,

you did it to me."

Matthew 25:40b

Imagine a sermon that begins: "Blessed are you poor. Blessed are those of you who are hungry. Blessed are those of you who are unemployed. Blessed are those going through marital separation. Blessed are those who are terminally ill."

The congregation does a double take. What is this? In the kingdom of the world, if you are unemployed, people treat you as if you have some sort of social disease. In the world's kingdom, terminally ill people become an embarrassment to our health-care system, people to be put away, out of sight. How can they be blessed?

The preacher responds, "I'm sorry. I should have been more clear. I am not talking about the way of the world's kingdom. I am talking about God's kingdom.

"In God's kingdom, the poor are royalty, the sick are blessed. I was trying to get you to see something other than that to which you have become accustomed."

. . . We can only act within a world we can see. Vision is the necessary prerequisite for ethics.

Stanley Hauerwas and William H. Willimon

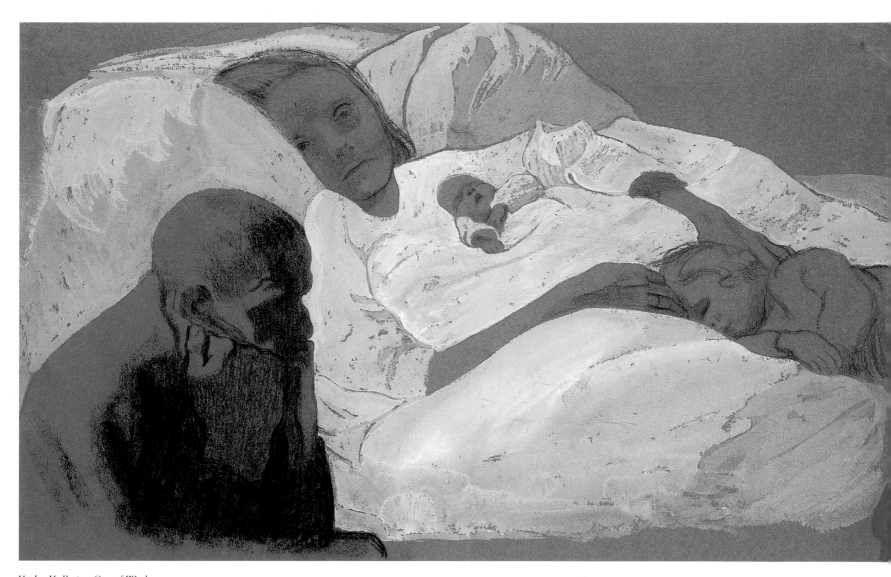

Käthe Kollwitz, *Out of Work*

Aaron Douglas, *Judgment Day*

The Judgment Day

And God will divide the sheep from the goats,
The one on the right, the other on the left.
And to them on the right God's a-going to say:
Enter into my kingdom.

Up and down the golden street,
Feasting on the milk and honey
Singing new songs of Zion,
Chattering with the angels
All around the Great White Throne.

. . .

And two by two they'll walk.

And to them on the left God's a-going to say:
Depart from me into everlasting darkness,
Down into the bottomless pit.
And the wicked like lumps of lead will start to fall,
Headlong for seven days and nights they'll fall,
Plumb into the big, black, red-hot mouth of hell,
Belching out fire and brimstone. . . .

James Weldon Johnson

Come, inherit the

for I was hungry

Gislebertus, *Last Judgment*, c. 1120–35, tympanum and lintel on the west portal, cathedral, Autun, France

On Christ's right are the righteous, accompanied by saints and angels. On Christ's left are the unrighteous souls being weighed and found wanting by the archangel Michael and being greeted by monstrous creatures on their way to hell. Artists of this period were not concerned about representing human forms naturalistically. Instead, they used distorted forms such as the ones above to express heightened emotion and meaning. As worshipers entered the cathedral, this scene reminded them in a compelling way of Christ's demand for righteous living.

kingdom, and you gave me food...

O God, who is old, and lives on fifty dollars a month, in one crummy room and can't get outside,
Help us to see you.

O God, who is fifteen and in the sixth grade,
Help us to see you.

O God, who is three and whose belly aches in hunger,
Help us to see you, as you have seen us in Jesus Christ our Lord.

O God, who sleeps in a bed with your four brothers and sisters, and who cries and no one hears you,
Help us to touch you.

O God, who has no place to sleep tonight except an abandoned car, an alley or deserted building,
Help us to touch you.

O God, who is uneducated, unskilled, unwanted, and unemployed,
Help us to touch you, as you have touched us in Jesus Christ our Lord.

. . .

O God, who is chased by the cops, who sits in jail for seven months with no charges brought, waiting for the Grand Jury and no money for bail,
Help us to know you.

. . .

O God, who is unorganized, and without strength to change your world, your city, your neighborhood,
Help us to join you.

O God, who is fed up with it all and who is determined to do something, who is organizing people for power to change the world,

Help us to join you, as you have joined us in Jesus Christ our Lord. Amen.

Robert W. Castle, Jr.

Salvador Dali, *Girl Standing at the Window*

Waiting, hoping, giving shape to our

dreams is part of the human condition.   To dream of a world of peace and justice, where God's goodness is all in

all, and to wake to its realization, is a cherished human hope. The figure

in Salvador Dali's *Girl Standing at the Window* waits with full attention for something. She looks expectantly out

into the wide world beyond her familiar harbor. Attentive, hope-filled, alert, with her whole being trained on the

horizon, she watches for the sign: the break in the meeting of sea and sky, the cloud of smoke that heralds

the messenger's arrival. Fully attentive—eyes and ears and imagination—she is ready to recognize and greet

a hope-filled future.

So the church waits for Jesus in Advent. Poised, we are alert to the signs of the times in nature, Scripture, news-

paper, ready to greet wherever the Christ appears. The Promise comes in unexpected peace blossoming like a

garden in winter, in the wake-up call of an unlikely prophet, in the sudden courage to risk bringing God's future

into being, in Mary's risk to bring Jesus into the world. Advent's color is deep blue, the color of the sky just

before the first rays of sunrise wake the rooster to announce to the watchers the dawning of the new day.

dvent

Full attention and imagination

KEEP AWAKE

Therefore, keep awake—for you know not when the owner of the house will come, in the evening, or at midnight, or at cockcrow, or at dawn, or else the owner may find you asleep when coming suddenly. And what I say to you I say to all: Keep awake."

Mark 13:35–37

A Song on the End of the World

On the day the world ends
A bee circles a clover,
A fisherman mends a glimmering net.
Happy porpoises jump in the sea,
By the rainspout young sparrows are playing
And the snake is gold-skinned as it
    should always be.

On the day the world ends
Women walk through the fields under
    their umbrellas,
A drunkard grows sleepy at the end of the lawn,
Vegetable peddlers shout in the street
And a yellow-sailed boat comes nearer the island,
The voice of a violin lasts in the air
And leads into a starry night.

And those who expected lightning and thunder
Are disappointed,
And those who expected signs of archangels'
    trumpets
Do not believe it is happening now,
As long as the sun and the moon are above,
As long as the bumblebee visits a rose,
As long as rosy infants are born
No one believes it is happening now.

Only a white-haired old man, who would be
    a prophet
Yet is not a prophet, for he's much too busy,
Repeats while he binds his tomatoes:
There will be no other end of the world,
There will be no other end of the world.

Warsaw, 1944
Czeslaw Milosz, translated by Anthony Milosz

The regularity of Christmas makes genuine expectancy difficult, at least for adults. Perhaps facing the unexpectedness of the ultimate divine invasion can lift believers above institutionalized expectations to a more vital watchfulness. Mark 13 speaks to those who expect too much and to those who expect too little. It is especially pertinent for those who have forgotten to expect anything at all.

Lamar Williamson, Jr.

Claudio Jimenez, *Festival Cross*

The cross used for fiestas celebrates the devoted life of Rosa Velasquez. Awakened by the cock's crow, all that follows in her day is touched by Christ.

Keep Awake, Be Always Ready

Words: Arthur G. Clyde, 1993

Tune: WACHET AUF, by Philipp Nicolai, 1599

1 Keep a-wake, be al-ways rea - dy, God's time ap-proach-es
2 Rise and shine for One is com - ing whose love will quench all

sure and stea - dy, God's strength will keep your heart from blame.
na-ture's thirst - ing to be made whole for - ev - er more.

Clouds, the Spir - it's light con-ceal - ing, dis - perse, God's pur - est
On that day to end all weep - ing, death's swords trans-formed to

light re - veal - ing; cre - a - tion will its Sov - ereign name. Dry
tools of reap - ing, the God of might will mer - cy pour. In -

branch - es burst forth green, God's ad - vent signs are
car - nate, God ap - pears em - brac - ing all our

seen: Hal - le - lu - jah! Christ's judg - ment won, God's
tears: Hal - le - lu - jah! God's maj - es - ty e -

will be done; God's new do - min - ion thus be - gun.
ter - nal - ly re - vealed to set the cos - mos free.

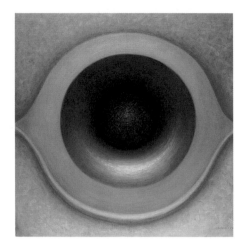

Rodolfo Abularach, *Cosmico Azul*

Darius and the Clouds

Darius, who doesn't like school,
who is sometimes stupid and mostly
a fool, said something wise today,
though most days he says nothing.
Darius, who chases girls with fire-
crackers or a stick that touched a rat
and thinks he's tough, today pointed
up because the world was full of
clouds, the kind like pillows.

You all see that cloud, the fat one
there? Darius said, See that? Where?
That one next to the one that look
like popcorn. That one there. See That.
That's God, Darius said. God?
somebody little asked. God, he said,
and made it simple.

Sandra Cisneros

For the Darkness of waiting
of not knowing what is to come
of staying ready and quiet and attentive,
we praise you, O God:
For the darkness and the light
are both alike to you.

. . .

For the darkness of hoping
in a world which longs for you,
for the wrestling and laboring of all creation
for wholeness and justice and freedom,
we praise you, O God:
For the darkness and the light
are both alike to you.

Janet Morley

Salvador Dali, *Girl Standing at the Window*

In contrast to the solidly framed window of the room from which the girl looks, the landscape onto which she looks leads away from her safe harbor to an unending vista of light and sea and sky.

Stir up our hearts, we beseech you, to prepare ourselves to receive your Son. When he comes and knocks, may he find us not sleeping in sin, but awake to righteousness, ceaselessly rejoicing in his love. May our hearts and minds be so purified, that we may be ready to receive his promise of eternal life.

The Gelasian Sacramentary, c. 500
This prayer is from what is possibly the oldest prayer book of the Western church.

GET READY

See, I am sending my messenger ahead of you, who will prepare your way; the voice of one crying out in the wilderness: 'Prepare the way of the Sovereign, make straight the Sovereign's paths.' "

Mark 1:2b–3

As long as we think
about John
like that
—preaching
in his own country
two thousand years ago—
his preaching
remains distant
and very far away.
Let us try
to get that wilderness
and also John's word
nearer home,
so that it can cut us
to the bone.
Let us speak
about the wilderness
in which we live.
And let us think
not only of sin
but of the world
we are accustomed
to.

Joseph G. Donders

Pieter Bruegel, the Elder, *Sermon of St. John the Baptist*

Bruegel set this painting of John the Baptist preaching in his own place and time, northern Europe in the sixteenth century.

repent

Wild the man and wild the place,
Wild his dress and wild his face,
Wilder still his words that trace
Paths that lead from sin to grace.

"Knock down every proud-backed hill!
Every canyon, valley fill!
Plane the soul and pray until
All its raucous rumblings still.

"Throw yourself in Jordan's streams,
plunge beneath each wave that gleams.
Wash away what only seems,
Rise and float on heaven's dreams.

"Leave on shore unneeded weight,
Fear and doubt, the skeptic's freight.
Toss them off and do not wait.
Time is short, the hour is late.

"One now comes whose very name
Makes my words seem mild and tame.
I use water to reclaim
Lives that he will cleanse with flame.

"You will see him soon appear:
One whose step through prayer you hear.
Christ is drawing, drawing near,
Christ is coming, coming here!"

Thomas H. Troeger

Pieter Bruegel, the Elder,
Sermon of St. John the Baptist, detail

Repentance is not passive waiting but active expectancy characterized by the alignment of one's whole being with what God is doing in the world. . . . "Repent," John insists, for repentance is the *sine qua non* for expectant watchfulness and for being received into the imminent reign of Yahweh. Thus repentant obedience is absolutely indispensable for the hopeful expectancy of Advent.

Richard D. N. Dickinson

The least we can do is to make his coming
not more difficult . . . than the earth makes it
for the spring when it wants to come.

Rainer Maria Rilke

Che Jesus,

They told me that you came back to be born every Christmas.
Man, you're crazy!
. . . with this stubborn gesture of coming back every Christmas
      you are trying to tell us something:

That the revolution that all proclaim begins first of all in
      each one's heart,
That it doesn't mean only changing structures but changing
      selfishness for love,
That we have to stop being wolves and return to being
      brothers and sisters,
That we . . . begin to work seriously for
individual conversion and social change
that will give to all the possibility of having bread,
education, freedom, and dignity.

That you have a message that's called the Gospel,
And a Church, and that's us—
A Church that wants to be servant of all,
A Church that knows that because God became human
      one Christmas
there is no other way to love God but to love all people.
If that's the way it is, Jesus, come to my house this Christmas,
Come to my country,
Come to the world of men and women.
And first of all, come to my heart.

Anonymous, Cordoba, Argentina, at Christmas, 1970

Diego Rivera, *The Offering*

This mural was painted as part of a government-sponsored mural
program in Mexico City during the 1920s. The mural has an almost
liturgical quality; it depicts a community, including those who carefully
prepare and offer the gifts as well as those who wait expectantly.

GOOD NEWS COMING

For as the earth brings forth its shoots,

and as a garden causes what is sown

in it to spring up, so the Sovereign God

will cause righteousness and praise to

spring up before all the nations.

Isaiah 61:11

Earth teach me stillness
    as the grasses are stilled with light.
Earth teach me suffering
    as old stones suffer with memory.
Earth teach me humility
    as blossoms are humble with beginning.
Earth teach me caring
    as the mother who secures her young.
Earth teach me courage
    as the tree which stands all alone.
Earth teach me limitation
    as the ant which crawls on the ground.
Earth teach me freedom
    as the eagle which soars in the sky.
Earth teach me resignation
    as the leaves which die in the fall.
Earth teach me regeneration
    as the seed which rises in the spring.
Earth teach me to forget myself
    as melted snow forgets its life.
Earth teach me to remember kindness
    as dry fields weep with rain.

Ute Prayer

Minnie Evans, *Untitled*

Minnie Evans used a wax crayon collage to produce a mosaic and dream-like design. Her art expressed the shimmering colors and religious quality that she discovered in the botanical garden where she worked.

Those mourning in Zion would possess new symbols of their status replacing the old symbols: flower garlands rather than ashes, oil to soothe the skin rather than mourning, mantles to wear rather than a fainting spirit. The consequences for those blessed would be a new status; they would be a new planting for a new day. In turn, the new status would bring a new task—the rebuilding of the cities and the restoration of the ruins to remove the results of years of devastation.

John Hayes

Senad Gubelic, *Child with Gun*

The smiling child's light grasp of the gun prevents its immediate use as a weapon. The photographer catches a moment of peace and creates a statement of hope.

noble

I would want a child to be with me.

powerful

If I were alone in a desert
   and feeling afraid,
I would want a child to be with me.
For then my fear would disappear
   and I would be made strong.
This is what life in itself can do
because it is so noble, so full of pleasure
   and so powerful.

Meister Eckhart

Spring Song

the green of Jesus
is breaking the ground
and the sweet
smell of delicious Jesus
is opening the house and
the dance of Jesus music
has hold of the air and
the world is turning
in the body of Jesus and
the future is possible

Lucille Clifton

Piet Mondrian,
Red Amaryllis with Blue Background

GREETINGS, FAVORED ONE!

he angel Gabriel came to Mary and said, "Greetings, favored one!

God is with you." But she was much perplexed by the words and

pondered what sort of greeting this might be. The angel said to her,

"Do not be afraid, Mary, for you have found favor with God.

And now, you will conceive in your womb and bear a son,

and you will name him Jesus."

Luke 1:28–31

You must be men and women of ceaseless hope, because only tomorrow can today's
human and Christian promise be realized; and every tomorrow will have its own
tomorrow, world without end. Every human act, every Christian act, is an act of hope.
But that means you must be men and women of the present, you must live this moment—
really live it, not just endure it—because this very moment, for all its imperfection and
frustration, *because* of its imperfection and frustration, is pregnant with all sorts
of possibilities, is pregnant with the future, is pregnant with love, is pregnant with Christ.

Walter J. Burghardt

Henry O. Tanner, *The Annunciation*

The light that surprises Mary conveys the mystery of the angelic greeting in Tanner's *Annunciation*.

This ancient anonymous work of the Eastern church was a sung litany. Its images communicate much of the Eastern church's teachings about Mary, drawing on images from the Hebrew Scriptures, the Gospels, and traditions of popular piety.

Hail, thou, the restoration of the fallen Adam;
hail, thou, the redemption of the tears of Eve.
Hail, heavenly ladder by which God came down;
hail, bridge leading from earth to heaven. . . .
Hail, land of promise;
     hail, thou from whom flows forth milk and honey.
Hail, space for the uncontained God;
     hail, door of solemn mystery.

"Selected Praises of Mary from the Agathestos Hymn,"
Greek, sixth century

FAVORED ONE

Paul Gauguin, *Ia Orana Maria (Hail Mary)*

Advent

They are fruit
and transport:
ripening melons,
prairie schooners journeying
under full sail.

Susan worries that her water will break
on the subway. New York is full of grandmothers;
someone will take care of her.
Kate has been ordered to bed.
A Wyoming wind like wild horses
brushes snow against her window.
Charlotte feels like a ripe papaya.
"The body's such a humble thing," she says,
afloat in her kitchen
in Honolulu,
unable to see her feet.

Pregnant women stand like sentinels,
they protect me
while I sleep. They part the sea
and pass down the bloody length of it,
until we are strangers
ready to be born,
strangers who will suffer and die.

They are home
and exile, beginning and end,
end and means.
I am more ordinary. Still, I listen
as the holy wind breathes through them.
I make a little song
in praise of bringing forth.

Kathleen Norris

Sing out my soul,

sing of the holiness of God:

who has delighted in a woman,

lifted up the poor,

satisfied the hungry,

given voice to the silent,

grounded the oppressor,

blessed the full-bellied
   with emptiness,

and with the gift of tears

those who have never wept;

who has desired the darkness
   of the womb,

and inhabited our flesh.

Sing of the longing of God,

sing out, my soul.

Janet Morley, based on Luke 1:39 – 53

Ethan Hubbard,
Young Woman of Costura, Guatemala

The young girl in this photograph is about
the age traditionally associated with Mary
at the time of the Annunciation.

Carmen Lomas Garza, *Posada (Inn)*

Christ

With worship, music, hospitality, gift-giving, believers greet

one another with the news of Jesus' birth. Jesus is born, Sun

of Righteousness, and the world is illumined by new light.   The church celebrates the birth of Jesus—the
                                                               Word of God—for twelve joyful days, wearing the
white and gold of a festival. With worship, music, hospitality, gift-giving, believers greet one another with the
news of Jesus' birth. The church's hope at this time is embodied in traditions such as the Mexican custom of
Las Posadas. As Christmas approaches, a procession of children and neighbors goes from house to house with
some of their members dressed as Mary, Joseph, and the angel. They call out for hospitality at each home, but
those within playfully make excuses and turn them away. The pilgrims persevere until the last house, when finally
the doors are opened and they and the whole procession are invited in. Families and friends welcome the travel-
ers with food, comfort, and celebration, hospitality not offered at the first Christmas.

Like Anna and Simeon in Luke's Gospel, wise ones among the church recognize that Jesus' birth fulfills their
hope that the long waiting time is over, and Emmanuel, God-with-us, is truly come. God's reign of justice and
peace has begun. Christians greet the Christ Child and others as bearers of this child, witnessing to the Word
among us.

mas

Welcome, welcome, Jesus Christ!

WELCOME, WELCOME, JESUS CHRIST!

When the angels had left them and gone into heaven, the shepherds said to one another, "Let us go now to Bethlehem and see this thing that has taken place, which God has made known to us." So they went with haste and found Mary and Joseph, and the child lying in the manger.

Luke 2:15–16

Georges de La Tour, *The Newborn Child*

Eucharistic Prayer for Christmas Eve

O Eternal Wisdom,
we praise you and give you thanks,
because you emptied yourself of power
and became foolishness for our sake:
for on this night you were delivered as one of us,
a baby needy and naked,
wrapped in a woman's blood;
born into poverty and exile,
to proclaim good news to the poor,
and to let the broken victims go free.

Therefore, with the woman who gave you birth,
the women who befriended you and fed you,
who argued with you and touched you,
the woman who anointed you for death,
the women who met you, risen from the dead,
and with all your lovers throughout the ages,
we praise you, saying:

Holy, holy, holy,
vulnerable God,
heaven and earth are full of your glory;
hosanna in the highest.
Blessed is the one
who comes in the name of God;
hosanna in the highest.

Blessed is our brother Jesus,
bone of our bone and flesh of our flesh;
who, on the night when he was delivered over to death,
took bread, gave thanks, broke it and said:
"This is my body, which is for you.
Do this to remember me."
In the same way also the cup, after supper, saying:
"This cup is the new covenant in my blood.
Do this, whenever you drink it,
to remember me."
For, as we eat this bread and drink this cup,
we are proclaiming the Lord's death until he comes.

Christ has died.
Christ is risen.
Christ will come again.

Come now, dearest Spirit of God,
embrace us with your comfortable power.
Brood over these bodily things,
and make us one body in Christ.
As Mary's body was broken for him,
and her blood shed,
so may we show forth his brokenness
for the life of the world,
and may creation be made whole
through the new birth in his blood.

Janet Morley

Joseph Stella, *The Crèche*

Carmen Lomas Garza, *Posada (Inn)*

Las Posadas, celebrated in Mexico and the Southwest United States, is a nine-day celebration of prayer in preparation for the feast of Christ's birth. Beginning on December 16, it ends at Midnight Mass (Mass of the Rooster) on Christmas Eve. During these days, processions of young "pilgrims," including Mary, Joseph, and the angel, go from house to house seeking shelter. Householders open their doors in welcome, and all the people in the procession are invited in to share the food which is offered in the home.

Welcome, welcome, Jesus Christ our infant savior,
baby who makes every birth holy.
May we, who like the shepherds
have witnessed in the stable a new kind of love,
return to our work with joy.
May we, for whom the heavens have opened
to proclaim that God is with us,
we who have fed on living bread
and drunk the wine of heaven,
go out to be instruments of your peace, day by day.

A New Zealand Prayer Book

THE WISE ONES

It had been revealed to Simeon by the Holy Spirit that he would not see death before he had seen God's Messiah. There was also a prophet, Anna. She was of a great age. She came, and began to praise God and to speak about the child to all who were looking for the redemption of Jerusalem.

Luke 2:26, 36a, 38

Eight days after the baby was born he was circumcised and he was called Jesus, because that was the name the angel had told Joseph to give him. . . .

How remarkable, how beyond the bounds of ordinary possibility, that two old people should see a small baby and recognize that he was the Light of the World! Was it perhaps because they were so old, so near to the Beyond, that they were able to see what people caught up in the cares of life could not see?

Madeleine L'Engle

Rembrandt Harmensz van Rijn, *The Presentation of Christ in the Temple*

Looking for Incarnation

*Gently, as if
passing treasured, fragile china dolls, they hand
their babies to me
there across the words
that make the time.
I splash the water
and look down for recognition.*

*I try to read those eyes to see if
something's there in
innocence that none yet
has taken note of,
something special from that
other side of being,
birth; a message
for us sinners gathered
round a bowl of water
and some ancient words.*

*"I baptize . . ." I begin
and think of Anna or
old Simeon, lifting up
a blushing Mary's baby,
all awash in wonder
to be holding God in hand.*

*The God who never tires
of birthing love in
this tired world came
once, a child.
I hold above the holy
water these new promises
that same God makes
to my world and wonder
if God's come again.*

Daniel H. Evans

Michael Freeman, *Shaker Woman*

From the Crag

You have granted me my full share of days,
The crown of old age—proud silver in my hair;
Hindsight to see clearly everywhere
From my crag, at the glint of memory:

The valley, the chasms through which I rode
With the chariots of my breaking dawn,
Through red summer, golden autumn,
To winter's white truth, when the wheels froze

The lines on my forehead from appreciated pain,
From passing through on your earth, suspecting your grace
Has everywhere stood by me and given solace

That just as your hand leads the sun into day
So too your hand strengthened my old wing,
Raised me to praise you from the crag where I cling.

Mani Leib

As a child I was told that grandfather spent an hour every morning and evening listening to God. So when I came suddenly upon my grandfather one day seated motionless in his armchair with closed eyes, I knew he was not asleep. He was talking with God. I stopped short where I was and stood very still. Perhaps if I listened intently enough I might hear God's voice speaking to my grandfather. But the room remained quiet, not even the faintest whisper reached my ears. After a long time my grandfather opened his eyes, saw me and smiled at me gently. These moments of intense listening for God's voice in the room with my grandfather are among the most vivid memories of my early childhood.

Helen Flexner

We were silent for a long time, lost in memories that the murmur of the mourning wind carried across the treetops. Cotton from the trees drifted lazily in the heavy air. The silence spoke, not with harsh sounds, but softly to the rhythm of our blood.

"What is it?" I asked, for I was still afraid.

"It is the *presence* of the river," Ultima answered.

I held my breath and looked at the giant, gnarled cottonwood trees that surrounded us. Somewhere a bird cried, and up on the hill the tinkling sound of a cowbell rang. The *presence* was immense, lifeless, yet throbbing with its secret message.

"Can it speak?" I asked and drew closer to Ultima.

"If you listen carefully—" she whispered.

"Can you speak to it?" I asked, and the whirling, haunting sound touched us.

"Ay, my child," Ultima smiled and touched my head, "you want to know so much."

Rudolfo A. Anaya

The child grew

and became strong,

filled with wisdom;

and the favor of God

was upon him.

Luke 2:40

Mev Puleo, *Presentation, Brazil*

Song of Simeon
(Nunc Dimittis)

Words: Luke 2:29–32
Transl. International Consultation of English Texts, 1975

Music: Ronald A. Nelson, 1986

CHILD, FULL OF GRACE

from the fullness

of the Child

have we all received,

grace upon grace.

John 1:16

divine

man

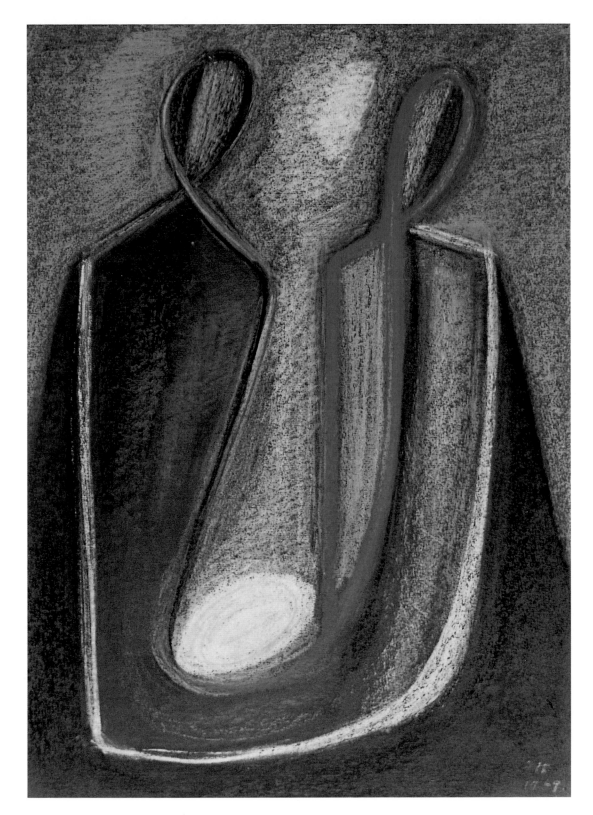

Jesus became flesh
so as to show forth the love
of God among us,
a love which is not merely
an expression of good will,
but the power of an
energy which is the heart,
core, and cohesive
force of the universe. . . .
Christ is the human expression
of God to us, and thus we
must try to understand
what God meant in Christ. . . .
Christ is not simply
the new male person,
but one who shows
all persons how to live.
As a human he shows us
what human self-possession
and self-giving are.
Thereby Christ shows us
the link between
divine and human,
the cosmos and its
conscious inhabitants.

Patricia Wilson-Kastner

Iris Hahs Hoffstetter, *We Saw His Glory*

The mystery of the Word becoming flesh
is imaged as light taking shape between
two abstract human figures.

Betty LaDuke, *Oregon: Jason's Journey*

Last Night

Last night, as I was sleeping,
I dreamt—marvelous error!—
that a spring was breaking
out in my heart.
I said: Along which secret aqueduct,
O water, are you coming to me,
water of a new life
that I have never drunk?

Last night, as I was sleeping,
I dreamt—marvelous error!—
that I had a beehive
here inside my heart.
And the golden bees
were making white combs
and sweet honey
from my old failures.

Last night, as I was sleeping,
I dreamt—marvelous error!—
that a fiery sun was giving
light inside my heart.
It was fiery because I felt
warmth as from a hearth,
and sun because it gave light
and brought tears to my eyes.

Last night, as I slept,
I dreamt—marvelous error!—
that it was God I had
here inside my heart.

Antonio Machado, translated by Robert Bly

Where he came from and who he was, he showed by what he taught and by the evidence of his life. He showed that he was the herald, the reconciler, our saviour, the Word, a spring of life and peace flooding over the whole face of the earth. Through him, to put it briefly, the universe has already become an ocean of blessings.

Clement of Alexandria

**Your heart goes out
to insignificant and little things,
to children, to the poor—
these are your kingdom.
For you became yourself
defenseless and humble,
resembling a human word,
a piece of bread, a name
that has to die.
We ask you then,
let us resemble you,
let us, imperfect as we are,
become your children,
your own beloved. . . .**

Huub Oosterhuis

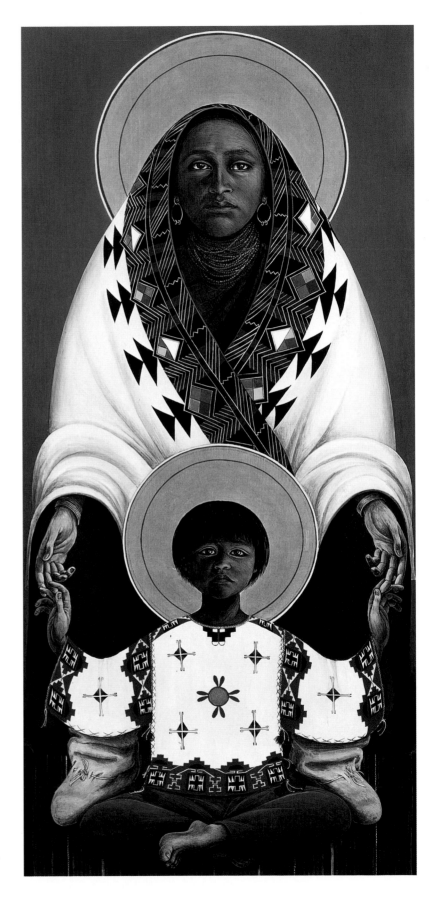

John Giuliani, *Hopi Mother and Child*

The particularity of the "Word made flesh"
is portrayed in this rendering of the traditional
Madonna and Child as Hopi Indians.

Jan Brueghel, the Elder, *Adoration of the Kings*, detail

Epiph

Extraordinary signs abound that transfigure ordinary occasions

and point to Jesus as God made manifest in the world.   Epiphany is the season of signs: it celebrates the manifestation to the world of God in Christ. Three foreign rulers travel far to see an ordinary Jewish baby; water becomes wine at Cana; the heavens open and the Spirit descends over Jesus' ritual bath in the Jordan. This One whom we recognize as one of us is God's own beloved.

The readings during this season remind us of God's persistence in calling us into a new, deeper relationship and sending us on a mission. Samuel is awakened in the night; Jonah is sent by boat—and great fish—to Nineveh. Isaiah's lyrical prophecies testify to God's power in the world, renewing the strength of the faithful to engage in God's ever-new project of justice and full life for all. The stories of Jesus reveal him acting with a new authority, casting out demons and restoring outcast sinners to fellowship.

The Feast of Transfiguration completes the season, when Jesus at prayer becomes radiant with light and communes with the prophets of God in whose tradition he stands. The Magi, the wedding guests at Cana, the Baptist, and the disciples who accompany Jesus to the mountaintop must read and interpret the signs about Jesus that the Spirit offers them in their lives. The contemporary church, standing in the tradition of these witnesses and followers of Christ, must seek the signs of Christ's presence in our midst as well. The church wears white at the festivals that begin and end this season; we wear the green of "ordinary time" during the heart of the season.

any

This One, one of us, is God's beloved

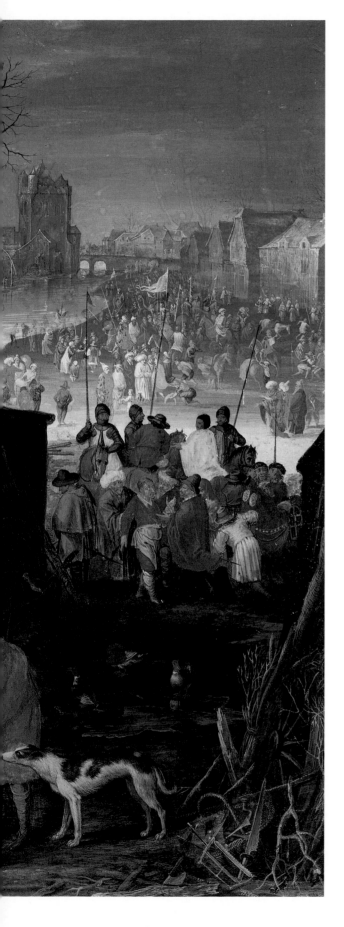

GIFT TO THE NATIONS,
GIFTS TO THE CHILD

Arise, shine; for your light has come,

and the glory of God has risen upon you.

And nations shall come to your light,

and rulers to the brightness of your rising.

They shall bring gold and frankincense,

and shall proclaim the praise of God.

Isaiah 60:1, 3, 6b

Jan Brueghel, the Elder, *Adoration of the Kings*

Jan Brueghel painted a biblical landscape where the Christ child draws
Brueghel's entire sixteenth-century Dutch world to the manger.

Aaron Douglas, *Rise, Shine, for Thy Light Has Come*

In choosing to be born for us,
God chose to be known by us.
God therefore reveals God's own
self in this way, in order that this
great sacrament of love may not
be an occasion for us of great
misunderstanding.

Today the magi find, crying
in a manger, the one they have
followed as he shone in the sky.
Today the magi see clearly,
in swaddling clothes, the one
they have long awaited as he
lay hidden among the stars.

Today the magi gaze in deep
wonder at what they see:
heaven on earth, earth in heaven,
humanity in God, God in humanity,
one whom the whole universe
cannot contain now enclosed
in a tiny body. As they look,
they believe and do not question
as their symbolic gifts bear witness:
incense for God, gold for a king,
myrrh for one who is to die.

Peter Chrysologus, 5th century

Jesus, as we travel far and fast,
lead our minds back to the [magi] following your star,
and forward to the day
when all see your shining light.

Jesus, light of the world,
let your bright star stand over the place
where the poor have to live;
lead our eager sages to wisdom and our rulers to reverence

O God, by the leading of a star
you revealed your Son Jesus Christ to the gentiles;
grant that your Church may be a light to the nations,
so that the whole world may come to see
the splendour of your glory;
through Jesus Christ our Lord.

A New Zealand Prayer Book

Jan Brueghel, the Elder, *Adoration of the Kings*, detail

God of gold, we seek your glory:

> **The richness that transforms our drabness into color,**
>
> **and brightens our dullness with vibrant light;**

your wonder and joy at the heart of all life.

God of incense, we offer you our prayer:

> **our spoken and unspeakable longings, our questioning of truth,**
>
> **our searching for your mystery deep within.**

God of myrrh, we cry out to you in our suffering:

> **The pain of all our rejections and bereavements,**
>
> **our baffled despair at undeserved suffering,**
>
> **our rage at continuing injustice;**

and we embrace you, God-with-us,

in our wealth, in our yearning, in our anger and loss.

Jan Berry

YOU ARE MY BELOVED

Just as Jesus was coming up out of the water, he saw the heavens torn apart and the Spirit descending like a dove on him. And a voice came from heaven, "You are my Child, the Beloved; with you I am well pleased."

Mark 1:10–11

The one who created us is waiting for our response to the love that gave us our being. God not only says: "You are my Beloved." God also asks: "Do you love me?" and offers us countless chances to say "Yes."

Henri Nouwen

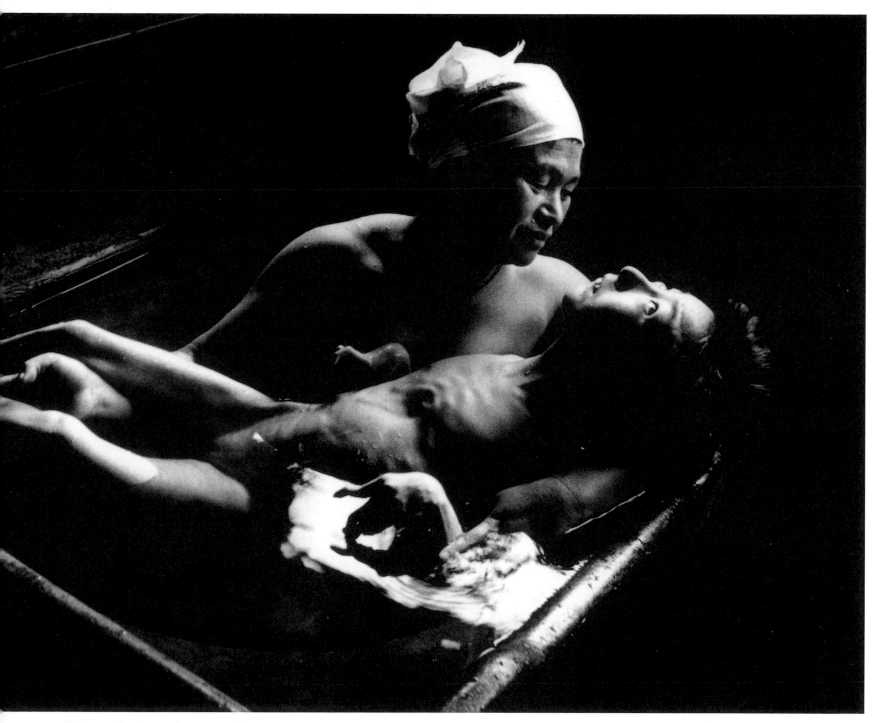

W. Eugene Smith, *Tomoko in Her Bath, Japan*

Smith's photograph, published in 1972 in *Life*, caused an international outcry against the industrial polluters whose careless environmental policies led to the severe birth defects suffered by Tomoko. Tomoko and her mother sharing the bath portrays complete intimacy, involvement, tenderness, and love.

John August Swanson, *The River*

Stepping in the Mud

The mud of human evil
    is very deep,
    it stinks forcefully,
    it is full of dangerous gases,
    and there was Jesus,
    in front of John,
    asking to be allowed
    to bend down in that mud.
    And John,
    no wonder,
    hesitated.
But he, Jesus,
he went down,
and when he came up,
the mud still streaming . . .
       HEAVEN OPENED,
    and a voice was heard . . .
    [and] a new Spirit
    a new life
    and a new heart
    were announced,
    glory, glory, alleluia.
He was bathed in light . . .
  drowned in God's voice . . .
  full of spirit;
    but what about the mud,
    was he going to forget it?
    . . . [No]
because once he got the spirit,
that Spirit drove him . . .
    to do his work
    in this world,
    to struggle with evil in us, . . .
    in this world,
    in order to overcome it.

Joseph Donders

The Negro Speaks of Rivers

I've known rivers:
I've known rivers ancient as the
    world and older than the flow
    of human blood in human veins.

My soul has grown deep like the rivers.

I bathed in the Euphrates when
    dawns were young.
I built my hut near the Congo and
    it lulled me to sleep.
I looked upon the Nile and raised
    the pyramids above it.
I heard the singing of the Mississippi
    when Abe Lincoln went down
    to New Orleans, and I've seen
    its muddy bosom turn all golden
    in the sunset.

I've known rivers:
Ancient, dusky rivers.

My soul has grown deep like the rivers.

Langston Hughes

What Ruler Wades through Murky Streams

Words: Thomas H. Troeger, 1984; rev. 1993   Music: WATER OF BAPTISM; David Hurd, 1994

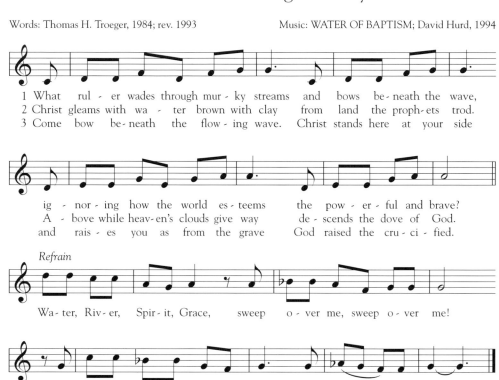

1 What rul-er wades through mur-ky streams and bows be-neath the wave,
2 Christ gleams with wa-ter brown with clay from land the proph-ets trod.
3 Come bow be-neath the flow-ing wave. Christ stands here at your side

ig-nor-ing how the world es-teems the pow-er-ful and brave?
A-bove while heav-en's clouds give way de-scends the dove of God.
and rais-es you as from the grave God raised the cru-ci-fied.

Refrain

Wa-ter, Riv-er, Spir-it, Grace, sweep o-ver me, sweep o-ver me!

Re-carve the depths your fing-ers traced in sculpt-ing me.

My soul has grown deep like the rivers.

Langston Hughes

John August Swanson, *The River*, detail

HERE I AM!

Now God came and stood there, calling as before, "Samuel! Samuel!"

And Samuel said, "Speak, for your servant is listening."

1 Samuel 3:10

Brother Eric de Saussure, *Samuel's Calling*, detail

As my prayer became more attentive and inward
I had less and less to say.
I finally became completely silent.
I started to listen
—which is even further removed from speaking.
I first thought that praying entailed speaking.
I then learnt that praying is hearing,
not merely being silent.
This is how it is,
To pray does not mean to listen to oneself speaking.
Prayer involves becoming silent,
and being silent,
and waiting until God is heard.

Sören Kierkegaard

Joshua Reynolds, *The Infant Samuel*

In a [somber] time
when prophetic utterance
was rare, [God] spoke
frequently to the young boy,
and his reputation spread
throughout Israel.

Eerdman's Bible Dictionary

Listen, my child, . . . with the ear of your heart.
Hearken to my words if you would have life!

St. Benedict, sixth century

Up in this high air,
you breathed easily,
drawing in a vital
assurance and lightness
of heart. In the highlands,
you woke up in the
morning and thought:
"Here I am, where I ought to be."

Isak Dinesen

Mev Puleo, *Girls Praying*

We are young despite the years.

We are concern.

We are hope despite the times.

R.E.M.

You wish to see; **Listen**

Hearing is a step toward **Vision**

St. Bernard of Clairvaux (1090–1153)

In the depth of silence
no words are needed,
no language required.
In the depth of silence
I am called to listen.

Listen to the beating of your heart.
Listen to the blowing of the wind,
the movement of the Spirit.
Be silent, said the Lord,
and know that I am God.

And listen to the cry of the voiceless.
Listen to the groaning of the hungry.
Listen to the pain of the landless.
Listen to the sigh of the oppressed
and to the laughter of children.

For that is authentic communication;
listening to people
living with people
dying for people.

An Indonesian author, 1983

Matthew Inglis, *Walls Have Ears*

Inglis employs ironic humor to comment visually on the technologies created by contemporary society
to enable people to "listen in" to events from all over the world.

THE WORD TO JONAH

T he word of God came to Jonah a second time, saying, "Get up, go to Nineveh, that great city, and proclaim to it the message that I tell you."

Jonah 3:1–2

The Prayer of Jonah
(or: the futility of hatred)

Out of my distress I called you, O Lord,
but you did not answer me.

I refused to preach repentance to the Ninevites,
but you forced me.
When I sailed away in the opposite direction,
you hurled a violent wind at me.
Your monster swallowed me and returned me to your path.

Repentance I would not preach in Nineveh,
rather I cursed them, "Forty days more and Nineveh shall be
destroyed."

But you did not listen to me.
You listened to the people of Nineveh as they sat in ashes
covered with sackcloth.

I am angry because you are a gracious and merciful God,
slow to anger,
rich in clemency,
loathe to punish.

If you will not destroy Nineveh then give me death.
It is better for me to die than to see my enemy live.

Thomas Reese

Albert Pinkham Ryder, *Jonah*

Howard Finster, *Nineveh (Garden Wall)*

Known as Paradise Garden, the former backyard of preacher and folk
artist Howard Finster celebrates the primary relationship between God
and humanity. On a wall, Finster portrays the repentant Ninevites.

A Fish Story from the Television Series
Northern Exposure

*Joel is fishing on a lake in Alaska at night and suddenly
imagines his rabbi from home in New York is with him.
They are inside a great fish.*

Rabbi Schulman: We're inside, Joel.

Joel: Inside what?

Rabbi Schulman: The fish . . . the belly of the beast
. . . You know, Jonah may be the
key here.

Joel: Key to what?

Rabbi Schulman: The meaning of all this. Think a
minute, Joel. Why was Jonah
swallowed in the first place?
[God] told him to go to Nineveh,
cry out against their wicked-
ness. Instead, Jonah flees, hops
a boat for Tarshish. [God] raises
a ruckus, Jonah gets the heave
ho. What's the message, Joel?

Joel: Next time go to Nineveh.

Rabbi Schulman: Responsibility. Jonah was trying to avoid his responsibility.

Jeff Melvoin

Paul Kittelson, *Whale*

Losers

If I should pass the tomb of Jonah
I would stop there and sit for awhile;
Because I was swallowed one time deep in the dark
And came out alive after all.

Carl Sandburg

A New Teaching

they were all amazed, and they

kept on asking one another,

"What is this? A new teaching—

with authority! Jesus commands

even the unclean spirits,

and they obey him."

Mark 1:27

Whether historical fact or symbol, Jesus' miracles are an essential part of his teaching (there are seventeen miracles in the first eight chapters of Mark, the earliest Gospel), and they are one of the ways he teaches; his miracles, in a sense, are like the parables manifested in the physical world. His audience was accustomed to the concept, for they were raised in a long tradition of miracles, many of them inextricably tied to the central teachings of Judaism.

Dan Wakefield

My battles are fought out inside, with my own demons.

Etty Hillesum

Edvard Munch, *The Scream*

Munch's image of the tormented screamer in the nightmarish landscape has become an icon of the terrors and isolation of modern-day life.

The image of Jesus as exorcist is someone who has experienced his own demons (Mark 1:12–13). The temptation stories point to the image of a wounded healer, to an image of one who by his own experience understands vulnerability and internalized oppression. In having recovered their own hearts, healers have some understanding of the suffering of others.

Naming the demons means knowing the demons. . . . The Gospels imply that anyone who exorcises cannot be a stranger to demons. . . . To have faced our demons is never to forget their power to hurt and never to forget the power to heal that lies in touching brokenheartedness. . . . Jesus hears, below the demon noises, an anguished cry for deliverance. Through . . . mutual touching, . . . community is cocreated as a continuing, liberating, redemptive reality.

Rita Nakashima Brock

Healing of the Possessed of an Evil Spirit, detail of ivory tablet, 11th century, Milan or Reichenau

The fear of the possessed man, the strength of the demon, the simplicity of Jesus' healing touch are graphically rendered in the work of this anonymous ivory carver.

Where a protest against human suffering takes place through a revelation of the sacred, the elimination of that suffering is not just desirable; it is not less than an obligation. . . . This is the final implication of the miracle stories: they will rather deny the validity of all previous experiences than the right of human suffering to be eliminated.

Gerd Theissen

We give praise and thanks to you, O God!
In Jesus Christ, you have given us life;
brought ministry, forgiveness, healing, and peace;
commanded the disciples to heal the sick;
and continued the healing ministry among us to this day.
Keep us mindful of your love and mercy
that we may be faithful
throughout all our days,
in the name of Jesus Christ.
Amen.

United Church of Christ Book of Worship

Linda Post, *Solstice*

WITH WINGS LIKE EAGLES

God gives power to the faint, and strengthens

the powerless. Even youths will faint and

be weary, and the young will fall exhausted;

but those who wait for God shall renew

their strength, they shall mount up with wings

like eagles, they shall run and not be weary,

they shall walk and not faint.

Isaiah 40:29–31

Ayako Araki, *Migrating Birds*

Araki, from northeast China, painted these birds after her first visit to Palestine. For her the birds expressed God's promise.

Cliff Bahnimptewa, *Kwahu (Eagle)*

The eagle is associated with divine power in some religions. The Hopi people find in the eagle a source of healing and lifegiving rain. The Eagle Katsina (dance) is an essential expression of that hope.

In circumstances where those in the best condition possible to humans *stumble and collapse* . . . , a special group runs on with new and greater vigor than before. They are *those waiting [hoping] on [God].* . . . Israel's impatience and insistence on prompt action from God could become [their] undoing. An attitude which can wait for the God of the ages and [God's] plan will gain *strength* to *rise* above the moment, *not tire* and *not faint,* but go on and on.

John D. W. Watts

Eagle Poem

To pray you open your whole self
To sky, to earth, to sun, to moon
To the one whole voice that is you.
And know there is more
That you can't see, can't hear
Can't know except in moments
Steadily growing, and in languages
That aren't always sound but other
Circles of motion.
Like eagle that Sunday morning
Over Salt River. Circled in blue sky
In wind, swept our hearts clean
With sacred wings.
We see you, see ourselves and know
That we must take the utmost care
And kindness on all things.
Breathe in, knowing we are made of
All this, and breathe, knowing
We are truly blessed because we
Were born, and die soon, within a
True circle of motion,
Like eagle rounding out the morning
Inside us
We pray that it will be done
In beauty
In beauty

Joy Harjo

A free bird leaps

on the back of the wind

and floats downstream

till the current ends

and dips his wings in the orange sun rays

and dares to claim the sky.

Maya Angelou, from "Caged Bird"

Religion and the Corruption of Faith

"I will go unto the altar of God." And the monk responded, "To God who gladdens my youth."

"*Juventutem meam,*" he said, distinctly and with feeling. My youth.

He was 81.

To those whose lives are fueled by belief— to people still young at 81 because they're scarcely at the threshold of eternity—there's no corner of life where faith is irrelevant.

Tony Proscio

Today, God, help me to let go of my need to do it alone and my belief that I am alone. Help me to tap into Your Divine Power and Presence, and Your resources for love, help, and support that's there for me. Help me know I am loved.

Melanie Beattie

Wilma Rudolph

Stretching for the tape in the 100-meter dash in the 1960 Olympics, Wilma Rudolph, disabled in childhood and unable to walk until the age of eight, won gold medals in the 100- and 200-meter dashes and as a member of the 400-meter relay team.

CLOTHED WITH JOY

You have turned my mourning into dancing;

you have taken off my sackcloth and clothed

me with joy, so that my soul may praise you

and not be silent. O Sovereign my God,

I will give thanks to you forever.

Psalm 30:11–12

[The psalmist] has changed the garment of penitence, worn round the body like sackcloth with a rope girdle, and been given a festive dress, in order to take part in a merry festal dance and this change of dress is the outward manifestation of the change that took place in the poet's soul when his prayer was granted.

Artur Weiser

Given a festive dress

Cathy Wilcox, *A Proper Little Lady*

For the world and time are
the dance of the Lord in
emptiness. The silence of the
spheres is the music of the
wedding feast. The more we
persist in misunderstanding
the phenomena of life,
the more we analyze them
out into strange finalities
and complex purposes of our
own, the more we involve
ourselves in sadness, absurdity
and despair. But it does not
matter much, because no
despair of ours can alter the
reality of things, or stain the
joy of the cosmic dance
which is always there.

Thomas Merton

Attributed to Auguste Rodin, *Dancer with Veils*

Women in Namibia Dancing
(Afrapix/Impact Visuals, N.Y.)

A dance of joy and empowerment
inspires the women of Namibia
to keep up their fight for full
freedom for women of
their country.

Lars Topelmann

Fount of all life, dancing in bliss,
Breaking down walls, making new space.

Burning up evil, creating fires,
Calling your people, follow in faith.

Living with Jesus, power in his Name,
Healing the broken, restoring the lame.

Casting out demons, raising the dead,
Calming life's storms, removing all dread.

Living to serve, confirmed from above,
Tested by fire, aflame with God's love.

Seeking the lost, sharing all pain,
Love at such cost, rising again.

Lighting our path, dancing ahead,
Leading through death, lifting to life.

United Theological College, Bangalore, India

Psalm 26

When the day comes on which our victory
will shine like a torch in the night,
it will be like a dream.
We will laugh and sing for joy.
Then the other nations will say about us,
"The Lord did great things for them."
Indeed, [God] is doing great things for us;
That is why we are happy in our suffering.

Lord, break the chains of humiliation and death,
just as on that glorious morning
when you were raised.
Let those who weep as they sow the seed of justice and freedom
gather the harvest of peace and reconciliation.

Those who weep as they go out as instruments of your love
will come back singing for joy,
as they witness the disappearance of hate
and the manifestation of love in your world.

Zephania Kameeta, Namibia

I WILL DO A NEW THING

I do not remember the former things, or consider the things of old. I am about to do a new thing; now it springs forth, do you not perceive it? I will make a way in the wilderness and rivers in the desert.

Isaiah 43:18–19

We are the children of the sun are we,
who write in the shadows of the evening,
who walk in the dark of the night,
who arise in the light of the dawn,
who go barefoot in the womb of the world,
who sow the field,
who grow the daily bread,
who know the language of the wind,
who see the rain fall on a parched land
and on tired faces,
who plough the furrows of the old,
who bring bones to bloom,
who consecrate bread in our flesh,
who break the chains and discover the way.

Michele Najilis, Nicaragua

Wilhelm Morgner, *Fields*

The words of judgment are over; God is now ready to do a new and totally different thing. The day of salvation is at hand.

The forthcoming salvation will be analogous to the Exodus: God will make a way through the wilderness between Babylonia and Palestine . . . just as God made a way through the sea when the Hebrews came out of Egypt.

Fred Craddock

I consider the human person
to be the irremovable
central place of the struggle
between the world's
movement away from God
and its movement towards
God. . . . Our age is intent
on escaping from the
demanding "ever anew."

Martin Buber

The Resurrection Window, First Presbyterian Church, Lisburn, Northern Ireland

The *Resurrection Window* is created out of shards of stained glass that were blown out of the original
windows at First Lisburn during a terrorist explosion at the height of the "troubles" in Northern Ireland.
The congregation decided to remain in their location and rebuild as a witness to their hope for peace
in Northern Ireland. The spiral of glass portrays a new sort of explosion—of God's power to bring peace.

May it come soon
to the hungry
to the weeping
to those who thirst for your justice,
to those who have waited centuries
for a truly human life.
Grant us the patience
to smooth the way
on which your Kingdom comes to us.
Grant us hope
that we may not weary
in proclaiming and working for it,
despite so many conflicts,
threats and shortcomings.
Grant us a clear vision
that in the hour of our history
we may see the horizon,
and know the way
on which your Kingdom comes to us.

Prayer for Nicaragua

Poetry will change your name,

you shall no longer be called

wounded, outcast, lonely or afraid.

I will change your name,

your new name shall be

confidence, joyfulness, overcoming one,

faithfulness, friend of God,

one who seeks my face.

D. J. Butler

I am about to do a new thing;
now it springs forth,

do you not perceive it?

IN LEVI'S HOUSE

As Jesus sat at dinner in Levi's house,

many tax collectors and sinners were also

sitting with Jesus and the disciples—

for there were many who followed him.

Mark 2:15

"Table fellowship"—sharing a meal with somebody—had a significance in Jesus' social world that is difficult for us to imagine. It was not a casual act, as it can be in the modern world. In a general way, sharing a meal represented mutual acceptance. More specifically, rules surrounding meals were deeply embedded in the purity system. Those rules governed not only what might be eaten and how it should be prepared, but also with whom one might eat. Refusing to share a meal was a form of social ostracism. Pharisees (and others) would not eat with somebody who was impure, and no decent person would share a meal with an outcast. The meal was a microcosm of the social system, table fellowship an embodiment of social vision.

Marcus J. Borg

Paolo Veronese, *The Feast at the House of Levi*

Famous for his opulent scenes of feasting drawn from Scripture, Veronese was called before the Inquisition to answer for the presence of "buffoons, drunkards . . . and similar vulgarities." With this untitled canvas, which the Inquisitors believed was a depiction of the Last Supper, Veronese successfully defended himself with an appeal to a kind of "artistic license"; he then gave the piece its title, which identifies the occasion as one where Jesus welcomes all manner of "vulgar" people.

We are your people:
Spirit of grace,
you dare to make us
Christ to our neighbors
of every culture and place.
Joined in community,

treasured and fed,
may we discover
gifts in each other,
willing to lead and be led.

Rich in diversity,
help us to live
closer than neighbors,
open to strangers,
able to clash and forgive.

Glad of tradition,
help us to see
in all life's changing,
where Christ is leading,
where our best efforts should be.

Give as we venture
justice and care
(Peaceful, insisting,
risking, resisting),
wisdom to know when and where.

Spirit, unite us,
make us, by grace,
willing and ready,
Christ's living body,
loving the whole human race.

Brian Wren

John Perceval, *Christ Dining in Young and Jackson's*

When the scribes of the Pharisees saw that he was eating with sinners
and tax collectors, they said to the disciples, "Why does Jesus eat
with tax collectors and sinners?" When Jesus heard this, he said to them,
"Those who are well have no need of a physician, but those who are sick;
I have come to call not the righteous but sinners."

Mark 2:15–17

Joined in community

I lived right here in this community my whole life and I guess I made myself a friend or two, they said I did anyhow, and folks turned out for my funeral, I'll say that for 'em. . . . Now if I'd just thought beforehand I would've told somebody to make my funeral long on singing and short on preaching. . . . It was a beautiful sermon, it really was, and about how I was still living Here on the other side in the bosom of Jesus, and how we could all meet again in Glory if only we was saved. Well, I hoped it made everybody's heart glad, because I knew it was true and *I* was glad to be living in the bosom of Jesus, but I don't know . . . Brother Packer went ahead and commenced to try and save everybody there at the church. Well, that didn't seem fitting to me, seeing as how about half the congregation was already members of the First Baptist anyhow.

I'll tell you something else—'course, I didn't know this when I was on the other side and I know they don't know it either—but They're a lot more lenient Here than I ever thought. Surprised me when I saw some of these Catholic I-talians I'd mined coal with down at Hughes hanging around when I first come over. But after while you start getting used to them being around and start seeing how if They didn't let none but the Baptists—or none but the Baptists and Church of Christs, say—come in, why, that'd leave a terrible number of lost souls crying around for eternity, and leave it be a little lonesome Here besides.

What I mean is, I might just as soon the preacher'd preached about the love of God and the bosom of Jesus and left off trying to save everybody in favor of music.

Rille Askew

People of God,
look about and see the faces of those
we know and love—
neighbors and friends,
sisters and brothers—
a community of kindred hearts.

People of God,
look about and see the faces
of those we hardly know—
strangers, sojourners, forgotten friends,
the ones who need an outstretched hand.

People of God,
Look about you and see all the images of God assembled here.
In me, in you, in each of us,
God's spirit shines for all to see.

People of God, come.
Let us worship together.

Ann Aspen Wilson

UPON A HIGH MOUNTAIN

*S*ix days later, Jesus took with him Peter and James and John,

and led them up a high mountain apart, by themselves.

And he was transfigured before them. Then a cloud

overshadowed them, and from the cloud there came a voice,

This is my Child, the Beloved; to this one you shall listen!"

Suddenly when they looked around, they saw no one

with them any more, but only Jesus.

Mark 9:2, 7–8

We of the Taizé community look upon the transfiguration above all as the celebration of that presence of Christ which takes charge of everything in us and transfigures even that which disturbs us about ourselves. God penetrates those hardened, incredulous, even disquieting regions within us, about which we really do not know what to do. God penetrates them with the life of the Spirit and acts upon those regions and gives them God's own face.

Kathryn Spink

Suddenly they saw him
    the way he was,
the way he really was
    all the time,
although they had never
    seen it before,
the glory which blinds
    the everyday eye
and so becomes invisible.
    This is how
he was, radiant, brilliant,
    carrying joy
like a flaming sun
    in his hands.
This is the way he was—is—
    from the beginning,
and we cannot bear it.
    So he manned himself,
came manifest to us;
    and there on the mountain
they saw him, really saw him,
    saw his light.
We all know that if we really
    see him we die.
But isn't that what is
    required of us?
Then, perhaps, we will see
    each other, too.

Madeleine L'Engle

Raphael, *Transfiguration*

Raphael combines in one painting the account of Jesus' transfiguration (Mark 9:2–8) with the account of Jesus healing a child possessed by a spirit (Mark 9:14–29). The transfiguration sends Jesus into the world to care for those who suffer.

František Kupka, *Madame Kupka among Verticals*

Ten years after the Czech artist painted Madame Kupka, František Kupka overpainted her portrait with vivid verticals, transforming the canvas and choosing to be faithful to his inner vision rather than to the model.

Once, as I rode out into the woods for my health, in 1737, . . . for divine contemplation and prayer, I had a view, that for me was extraordinary, of the glory of the Son of God, as Mediator between God and [humanity], and his wonderful, great, full, pure and sweet grace and love, and meek and gentle condescension. This grace that appeared so calm and sweet, appeared also great above the heavens. The person of Christ appeared ineffably excellent, with an excellency great enough to swallow up all thought and conception—which continued, as near as I can judge, about an hour; which kept me the greater part of the time, in a flood of tears, and weeping aloud. I felt an ardency of soul to be, what I know not otherwise how to express, emptied and annihilated; to lie in the dust, and to be full of Christ alone; to love him with a holy and pure love; to trust in him; to live upon him; to serve and follow him; and to be perfectly sanctified and made pure, with a divine and heavenly purity.

Jonathan Edwards (1703–1758)

Elijah Pierce, *The Transfiguration*

Follow me...

In Alice Walker's short story "The Welcome Table," an old woman banned from church because she disrupts the others from their ardent prayers has her own transfiguring experience, her death depicted as a long walk with Jesus. Jesus' silent presence and attention bring her happiness and peace.

All he said when he got up close to her was "Follow me," and she bounded down to his side with all the bob and speed of one so old. . . . They walked along in deep silence for a long time. Finally she started telling him about how many years she had cooked for them, cleaned for them, nursed them. . . . She told him indignantly about how they had grabbed her when she was singing in her head and not looking, and how they had tossed her out of his church. . . . A old heifer like me, she said, straightening up next to Jesus, breathing hard. But he smiled down at her and she felt better instantly and time just seemed to fly by. When they passed her house, forlorn and sagging, weatherbeaten and patched, by the side of the road, she did not even notice it, she was so happy to be out walking along the highway with Jesus.

She broke the silence once more to tell Jesus how glad she was that he had come . . . and how she never expected to see him down here in person. Jesus gave her one of his beautiful smiles and they walked on. She did not know where they were going; someplace wonderful, she suspected. The ground was like clouds under their feet, and she felt she could walk forever without becoming the least bit tired. She even began to sing out loud some of the old spirituals she loved, but she didn't want to annoy Jesus, who looked so thoughtful, so she quieted down. They walked on, looking straight over the treetops into the sky, and the smiles that played over her dry wind-cracked face were first clean ripples across a stagnant pond. On they walked without stopping.

Alice Walker

Betty LaDuke, *Guatemala: Procession*

Jesus, calling people to "follow me,"

now leads his followers into the heart

of the world's suffering and struggle. The image of the Palm Sunday procession captures the imagination of
the church in Lent. Jesus, who began his ministry by calling people to
"follow me," now leads his followers into the heart of the world's suffering and struggle. Confronting the power
of sin manifest in individuals and in society, Jesus preaches freedom, healing, justice, and new life. To follow
Jesus means to carry out his mission in our time: it requires humble self-knowledge and the willingness to
change one's own life. It requires, as well, confident courage to confront the world to change its sinful structures. "Follow me" extends to Jerusalem where Jesus is hailed as ruler, then on to Calvary where he faces death.
Jesus promises no safety along the road; he promises only to provide those who follow with "the Way, the truth,
and the life."

Covenant with a faithful God forms the context for this year's Lenten journey. The Hebrew Scriptures offer
reminders of God's promises of life and relationship made to Noah and his family, Abraham and Sarah, and
Jeremiah. Christians experience God's covenant faithfulness continuing in Jesus—God-with-us—who shares our
life and our death. Lent begins with the black and gray of Ash Wednesday; it ends with the red of Good Friday.
Along the way the church wears purple, a color long associated with penitence.

Lent
Following even to Jerusalem

Yet even now," says God,

"return to me with all your heart,

with fasting, with weeping,

and with mourning; and rend your

hearts and not your garments."

Return to your God, for God

is gracious and merciful, slow

to anger, and abounding in steadfast

love, and repents of evil."

Joel 2:12–13

What the Living Do

John, the kitchen sink has been clogged for days,
    some utensil probably fell down there.
And the Drano won't work but smells dangerous,
    and the crusty dishes have piled up

waiting for the plumber I still haven't called.
    This is the everyday we spoke of.
It's winter again: the sky's a deep, headstrong blue,
    and the sunlight pours through

the open living-room windows because the heat's
    on too high in here and I can't turn it off.
For weeks now, driving, or dropping a bag of groceries
    in the street, the bag breaking,

I've been thinking: This is what the living do.
    And yesterday, hurrying along those
wobbly bricks in the Cambridge sidewalk, spilling my coffee
    down my wrist and sleeve,

I thought it again, and again later when buying a hairbrush:
    This is it.
Parking. Slamming the car door shut in the cold.
    What you called *that yearning*.

What you finally gave up. We want the spring to come
    and the winter to pass. We want
whoever to call or not call, a letter, a kiss—we want more and more
    and then more of it.

But there are moments, walking, when I catch a glimpse
    of myself in the window glass,
say, the window of the corner video store, and I'm gripped
    by a cherishing so deep

for my own blowing hair, chapped face, and unbuttoned coat
    that I'm speechless:
I am living. I remember you.

Marie Howe

Georges de La Tour,
The Penitent Magdalen

Although we now realize that
Mary Magdalen's image as a great
sinner or reformed prostitute
has been based on a confusion
of images with other women
in the New Testament, nevertheless
the legends of her great sorrow out
of love for Jesus have compelled
the imagination of artists who have
looked to her for images of repentance.
Georges de La Tour employs the
symbols of mortality, the skull and
self-examination, the mirror.

El Posito (Little Well of Healing Dirt) at Sanctuario de Chimayo, New Mexico

On the High Road between Sante Fe and Taos, New Mexico, is the village of Chimayo, a pilgrimage site invested with the traditions of Hispanic Catholicism. Here, at a shrine dedicated to Jesus, Our Lord of Esquipulas, is located a small dry well that is reputed to have healing qualities. People from around the world visit this shrine to "wash" themselves with this healing dirt and to carry some home to their families. In the small room by the well, as a thanksgiving offering they leave behind crutches and pictures of themselves healed.

**Would you become a pilgrim
on the road of Love?
The first condition is that
you make yourself
humble as dust and ashes.**

Ansarit of Herat

Come, brothers and sisters, let us consider the dust and ashes of which we were formed. What is the reality of our present life and what shall we become tomorrow? In death where is the poor and where the rich? Where is the slave and the master? They are all ashes. The beauty of countenance has withered, and the strength of youth has been cut down by death. . . . All has withered as the grass of the field and has vanished. Come . . . let us fall on our knees in humble prayer before Christ.

"Verses During the Last Kiss: Funeral of the Dead" (Orthodox Liturgy)

Psalm 103

Repeat. Do you read? Do you read?

    Are you in trouble?

    How did you get in trouble?

    If you are in trouble, have you sought help?

    If you did, did help come?

    If it did, did you accept it? Are you out of trouble?

    What is the character of your consciousness?

    Are you conscious?

    Do you have a self?

    Do you know who you are?

    Do you know what you are doing?

    Do you love?

    Do you know how to love?

    Are you loved? Do you hate?

    Do you read me?

Come back. Repeat. Come back. Come back. Come back.

Walker Percy

Barnett Newman, *First Station*

This minimalist painting consists of few elements or forms. Because of that, the viewer focuses on only one detail—shape, color, or space. Ash Wednesday focuses on the essential—ash and dust, life and death.

Remember, human, that you are dust, and to dust you will return.

From the Ash Wednesday liturgy, based on Genesis 3:19

RAINBOW PROMISE

Signs

If of seas and hills we continue to sing,
If somehow we think of all kinds of things,
If there still be some who with many colors paint,
Then perhaps together these are signs and more:
A sign that overhead the sun will still rise,
A sign that lilies will bloom white as before,
A sign that again the fields will be only green
And the skies not covered with clouds of red.

If yesterday we closed the shelters up, . . .
If these be not tears but the wetness of rain,
And the street-lamps glowing once again—
It is a sign that we may yet find the golden mean,
A sign that from now on forever we will only love,
A sign that one night a full moon will shine above—
And the Peace we have been seeking
will be back on the scene.

Havatslet Levi

God said, "I establish my covenant with you, that never again shall all flesh be cut off by waters of a flood, and never again shall there be a flood to destroy the earth." God said, "This is the sign of the covenant that I make between me and you and every living creature that is with you, for all future generations: I have set my bow in the clouds, and it shall be a sign of the covenant between me and the earth."

Genesis 9:11–13

God's Covenant

The covenant in Genesis 9:8–17 is dramatically distinctive in several ways: . . . it is made between God and all future generations . . . it is made not only with human beings but also with all creatures of the earth . . . and, most dramatic of all, only one party to the agreement—God—speaks at all. The covenant with Noah . . . is an act of a free and gracious God in behalf of a world that did not have to ask for it or earn it, or even respond to it.

John H. Hayes

Noah's Prayer

Lord,
what a menagerie!
Between Your downpour and these
   animal cries
one cannot hear oneself think!
The days are long,
Lord.
All this water makes my heart sink.
When will the ground cease to rock under
   my feet?
The days are long.
Master Raven has not come back.
Here is Your dove.
Will she find us twig of hope?
The days are long,
Lord.
Guide Your Ark to safety,
some zenith of rest,
where we can escape at last
from this brute slavery.
The days are long,
Lord.
Lead me until I reach the shore of Your
   covenant.
Amen

Carmen Bernos De Gasztold

God of the Sparrow God of the Whale

God of the sparrow
God of the whale
God of the swirling stars
How does the creature say Awe
How does the creature say Praise

God of the rainbow
God of the cross
God of the empty grave
How does the creature say Grace
How does the creature say Thanks

Jaroslav J. Vajda

**Lord,
what a menagerie!**

Barbara Reid, *With hoot and squawk and squeak and bark . . . The animals tumbled off the ark*

AN EVERLASTING COVENANT

I will make you exceedingly fruitful; and I will make

nations of you, and rulers shall come from you.

I will establish my covenant between me and you,

and your offspring after you throughout their

generations, for an everlasting covenant, to be

God to you and to your offspring after you.

Genesis 17:6–7

*The initiative
for the establishment
of the covenant
comes from God.
Among the promises
granted to Abraham
and Sarah and
their descendants,
the divine affirmation
"I will be their God"
stands out. That is not
a stipulation . . .
but states the essence
of the covenant itself.*

Fred Craddock

Illuminated manuscript, *Abraham Holding in His Lap His Descendants: Jews, Christians, and Muslims*

Me and you must never part.

Me and you must have one heart.

Ain't no ocean, ain't no sea,

Keep my sister away from me.

Me and you must never part.

Me and you must have one heart.

The Color Purple, book by Alice Walker, screenplay by Menno Meyjes

"I am looking for friends," [said the little prince]. "What does that mean—'tame?'"

"It is an act too often neglected," said the fox. "It means to establish ties."

"'To establish ties'?"

"Just that," said the fox. "To me, you are still nothing more than a little boy who is just like a hundred thousand other little boys. And I have no need of you. And you, on your part, have no need of me. To you, I am nothing more than a fox like a hundred thousand other foxes. But if you tame me, then we shall need each other. To me, you will be unique in all the world. To you, I shall be unique in all the world. . . ."

The fox gazed at the little prince, for a long time.

"Please—tame me!" [said the fox].

"I want to, very much," the little prince replied. "But I have not much time. I have friends to discover, and a great many things to understand."

"One only understands the things one tames," said the fox. "[People] have no time to understand anything. They buy things ready made at the shops. But there is no shop where one can buy friendship. . . . If you want a friend, tame me."

Antoine de Saint-Exupéry

Film still from *The Color Purple*

The young sisters, Celie and Nettie, promise each other in their childhood game a loving faithfulness that lasts their lifetime, enduring even separation.

Barbara Hepworth,
Figure (Merryn)

The curves of Hepworth's
sculpture suggest an unending
circle: complete and serene,
symbol of covenant promises.

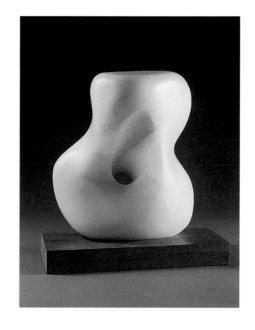

Exchange of Wedding Symbols

By these rings
of covenant promise,
Gracious God,
remind bride and
groom of your
encircling love and
unending faithfulness that
in all their life together
they may know joy and
peace in one another.

United Church of Christ Book of Worship

A Covenant Prayer in the Wesleyan Tradition

I am no longer my own, but thine.

Put me to what thou wilt, rank me with whom thou wilt.

Put me to doing, put me to suffering.

Let me be employed by thee or laid aside for thee,

exalted for thee or brought low by thee.

Let me be full, let me be empty.

Let me have all things, let me have nothing.

I freely and heartily yield all things

to thy pleasure and disposal.

And now, O glorious and blessed God,

Father, Son, and Holy Spirit,

thou art mine, and I am thine. So be it.

And the covenant which I have made on earth,

let it be ratified in heaven. Amen

The United Methodist Hymnal

In the temple Jesus found people selling.

He poured out the coins of the money

changers and overturned their tables.

Jesus told those who were selling,

"Take these things our of here! Stop

making God's house a marketplace!"

John 2:14a, 15b–16

Anger is a mode of connectedness to others and it is always a vivid form of caring. To put it another way: anger is —and it always is—a sign of some resistance in ourselves to the moral quality of the social relations in which we are immersed. . . . A chief evidence of the grace of God— which always comes to us in, with, and through each other— is the power to struggle and to experience indignation.

Beverly Harrison

Jesus' action in cleansing the temple precincts seems to [be] . . . a protest like that of the prophets of old against the profanation of God's house and a sign that the messianic purification of the Temple was at hand.

Raymond E. Brown

El Greco, *Cleansing the Temple*

"Woe to him whom this world charms from Gospel duty! Woe to him who seeks to pour oil upon the waters when God has brewed them into a gale! Woe to him who seeks to please rather than to appall! Woe to him whose good name is more to him than goodness! Woe to him who, in this world, courts not dishonor! Woe to him who would not be true, even though to be false were salvation! Yea, woe to him who, as the great Pilot Paul has it, while preaching to others is himself a castaway!"

Father Mapple of the Whaleman's Church in Herman Melville's *Moby Dick*

Mev Puleo, *Say No to Drugs*

A Just Anger

Anger shines through me.
Anger shines through me.
I am a burning bush.
My rage is a cloud of flame.
My rage is a cloud of flame
in which I walk
seeking justice
like a precipice.
How the streets
of the iron city
flicker, flicker,
and the dirty air
fumes.
Anger storms
between me and things,
transfiguring,
transfiguring.
A good anger acted upon
is beautiful as lightening
and swift with power.
A good anger swallowed,
a good anger swallowed
clots the blood
to slime.

Marge Piercy

We believe in Jesus Christ,
our saviour and liberator,
the expression of God's redeeming
and restoring love,
the mark of humanness,
source of courage, power and love,
God of God,
light of light,
ground of our humanity.

We believe that God resides in slums,
lives in broken homes and hearts,
suffers our loneliness, rejection and powerlessness.

But through death and resurrection
God gives life, pride and dignity,
provides the content of our vision,
offers the context of our struggle,
promises liberation
to the oppressor and the oppressed,
hope to those in despair. . . .

We believe in the activity of the Holy Spirit
who revives our decaying soul,
resurrects our defeated spirits,
renews our hope of wholeness
and reminds us of our responsibility
in ushering God's new order here and now.

Yong Ting Jin, Hong Kong

For God so loved the world that God gave God's only Child, so that everyone who believes in that Child should not perish but have eternal life. For God sent the Child into the world, not to condemn the world, but that through the Child the world might be saved.

John 3:16–17

Psalm 132
Jesus Is Love

Jesus is love
because God is love
Jesus is love
because God so loved the world
that Jesus was sent in love
for love
Jesus is love
breaks open the eternal possibility
for love
to be for all
because Jesus is love.

Benjamin F. Chavis, Jr.

God does not just deal with this world, but deals with it passionately, loving it and suffering for it. "God loved the world so much that he gave his only son to it" (John 3:16). But this is not logic. This is passion. How else would God be willing to part with God's own son for the sake of us? Nor is this a result of reasoning. It is a risk. And passion always involves risk, does it not? But only in risking will there be new discoveries and exciting experiences.

Choan-Seng Song

Ding Fang, *Go into Belief*

The outstretched offering of one takes on universal proportions in this Chinese painting.

Arms are spread wide with the world suspended above the figure.

The incarnation means therefore above all things that nothing—literally nothing—that happens in human life and in the world here and now can be regarded as having no relationship with God. The world is God's and God is in the world. All men and women are God's people and God is in us all—God near us, God with us, God in us, Immanuel.

Choan-Seng Song

I grew agitated each time he touched on the suffering of Jesus. For a long time my agitation confused me. I am a great lover of Jesus, and always have been. Still, I began to see how the constant focus on the suffering of Jesus alone excludes the suffering of others from one's view. . . . I knew I wanted my own suffering, the suffering of women and little girls, still cringing before the overpowering might and weapons of the torturers, to be the subject of a sermon. Was woman herself not the tree of life? And was she not crucified? Not in some age no one remembers, but right now, daily, in many lands on earth?

Alice Walker

My Bath

My bath is the ocean
and I am a continent
with hills and valleys
and earthquakes and storms.
I put the two mountain peaks of my knees
under water and bring them up again.

Our earth was like that—
great churnings and splashings,
and continents appearing and disappearing.

Only you, O God, know about it all,
and understand, and take care
of all creation.

Madeleine L'Engle

The best way to know God
is to love many things.

Vincent van Gogh

Keith Haring, *Altarpiece: The Life of Christ*

Keith Haring combines his pop figures with the style of ancient Russian icons. In the altarpiece he conveyed his interpretation of Christ—a cross, a glowing heart, a baby nested in arms, with blessings flowing down equally on all humankind. This last work of love and resurrection was completed two weeks before Haring's death from AIDS.

THE LAW WITHIN

I will put my law within them, and I will write it on their hearts; and I will be their God, and they shall be my people.

Jeremiah 31:33b

Charles White, *The Prophet #1*

The rose is often used as a symbol of perfection, and thus of God. This prophet's gaze upon the rose seems to suggest a life centered around the holy.

What then is new about the new covenant? That God initiates the covenant, that God forgives sins, and that Israel will "know" [God] intimately had been features of older covenants. What is without precedent is the law written on the heart, the covenant at the core of one's being. The newness is a special gift, the capacity to be faithful and obedient. In the Old Testament, the heart is the seat of the will . . . ; consequently, the special gift here is a will with the capacity to be faithful. God thus promises to change the people from the inside out, to give them a center. This covenant will overcome the conflict between knowing and wanting one thing and doing another. In the new covenant the people will act as if they are owned by God without even reflecting upon it.

Fred Craddock

How will the thousands

be shepherded

as I have shepherded thee?

Only if the eye of God

opens in the heart

of every[one]; if each will …

choose the way of life not death.

Arthur Miller

Psalm 51:10–12

Create in me a clean heart, O God,

and put a new and right spirit within me.

Cast me not away from your presence,

and take not your holy Spirit from me.

Restore to me the joy of your salvation,

and uphold me with a willing spirit.

Which laws, then,
are written
on the heart?
All the laws
of Moses?
Just the Decalogue?
The answer is
all of these things,
and none of them.
Just these words
will suffice:
"I am yours, and
you are mine,"
says [God].
That is the language
of love and
faithfulness.

Fred Craddock

Marc Chagall, *Klageleid des Jeremias*

Chagall's image of Jeremiah embraces his Torah scroll in a way which suggests he is taking it intimately "to heart."

JERUSALEM

Then those who went ahead and those who followed

were shouting, "Hosanna! Blessed is the one who comes

in the name of God! Blessed is the coming dominion

of our ancestor David! Hosanna in the highest heaven!"

Then Jesus entered Jerusalem and went into the temple.

Mark 11:9–11a

*From the village
of Bethany to
the city of Jerusalem
was scarely
half an hour's walk.
Moving from the
village and across the
Mount of Olives,
a twist in the
road revealed as
if by magic
a panoramic view
of the dun-brown
holy city within
its fortified walls. . . .
All along the
valley and all
across the lower
slope of Mount Olivet
stirred the masses
of pilgrims who
had come for the
Passover festival.*

Shusako Endo

Max Beckmann, *Landscape, Cannes*

I write this on a day given to remembering the triumphant entry of Christ into Jerusalem. This year the day seems empty and abstract. The events of the week are too overpowering. The knowledge that Christ's entry led directly to his Crucifixion looms too [grimly] ahead. This seems the strangest holiday of the year, a celebration of misunderstanding. In this world, the [dominion] has not yet come, though our hearts long for it and our lives incline toward it.

John Leax

The *Pesach* (Passover) was at hand. The people preparing for the festival were looking back on their long history, rueful over the anguished adversity of their ancient wandering migrations, and they prayed with fervor that God would come again to restore prosperity to his land now trampled underfoot by the Gentiles. Jesus, of course, knew the spirit of the feast. On this particular day, shortly before the festival itself began, with full knowledge he dared to plunge into that whirlpool of popular misunderstanding. Descending from the Mount of Olives and through the cheers from the crowd, he certainly knew that he was soon going to disappoint these people, and that the people in their frustration would then turn against him. . . . Jesus, coming down the mountain and entering the city, wore a painful smile.

Shusako Endo

Eliot Porter, *Christ's Entry into Jerusalem*, Church of Ixtepec, Oaxaca, Mexico

This *santos* (statue) is probably used in Palm Sunday processions each year in this parish.

Like splendid palm branches,

we are strewn in the Lord's path.

Latin antiphon

Betty LaDuke, *Guatemala: Procession*

All those who die like Jesus,

sacrificing their lives out of love

for the sake of a more dignified human life,

will inherit life in all its fullness.

They are like grains of wheat,

dying to produce life,

being buried in the ground

only to break through and grow.

Leonardo Boff

Jesus' awareness of his impending death permeates his actions and can be compared, I believe, to the knowledge held today by the terminally ill. . . . Jesus on Palm Sunday may be likened to the cancer patient who celebrates an anniversary—fully aware of the "lastness" of it all, yet celebrating nonetheless.

Lucy Bregman

Jesus, when you rode into Jerusalem

the people waved palms

with shouts of acclamation.

Grant that when the shouting dies

we may still walk beside you even to a cross. . . .

A New Zealand Prayer Book

Do You Know What I Have Done?

Now before the festival of Passover, Jesus knew that his hour had come to depart from this world and go to God. And during supper Jesus, knowing that God had given all things into his hands, and that he had come from God and was going to God, got up from the table, took off his outer robe, and tied a towel around himself. Then he poured water into a basin and began to wash the disciples' feet.

John 13:1a, 3–5a

Salvador Dali, *The Last Supper*

Earth, air, light, and water—all basic to life—converge in the bread and cup before Jesus.

The Washing of the Feet, (Vie de Jesus Mafa)

After Jesus had washed their feet, had put on his robe,

and had returned to the table, he said to them,

"Do you know what I have done to you?"

John 13:12

The Last Supper and Washing of Feet, French Psalter, 1260

Elements from many gospel "table scenes," including the Last Supper, are found in this medieval image.

God, food of the poor;
Christ, our bread,
give us a taste of the tender bread
from your creation's table;
bread newly taken from your heart's oven,
food that comforts and nourishes us.
A loaf of community that makes us human,
joined hand in hand, working and sharing.
A warm loaf that makes us a family;
sacrament of your body,
your wounded people.

Workers in community soup kitchens in Lima, Peru

The Foot-Washing

"I wouldn't take the bread and wine
if I didn't wash feet."
Old Regular Baptist

They kneel on the slanting floor
before feet white as roots,
humble as tree stumps.
Men before men
women before women
to soothe the sourness
bound in each other's journeys.
Corns, calluses, bone knobs
all received and rinsed
given back clean
to Sunday shoes and hightops.

This is how to prepare for the Lord's Supper,
singing and carrying a towel
and a basin of water,
praying while kids put soot
in their socks—almost as good
as nailing someone in the outhouse.
Jesus started it: He washed feet
after Magdalen dried His ankles
with her hair. "If I wash thee not,
thou hast no part with me."
All servants, they bathe
flesh warped to its balance. . . .
Lord of the bucket in the well.

George Ella Lyon

BY YOUR CROSS

My God, my God, why have you forsaken me?

Why are you so far from helping me,

from the words of my groaning? O my God,

I cry by day, but you do not answer;

and by night, but find no rest.

Psalm 22:1–2

*Because of the unity
of divinity
in the crucified Christ,
the God who is
self-giving and receiving
accepts the fragment
human condition
into the divine life for
healing, and the
humanity of Christ
gathers into himself
all the forces of alienation
and destruction
active in his own death.*

*All the dualisms
which divide, separate,
cause pain, and support
oppression and lack
of communion
with the others are all
gathered together
at the crucifixion,
and Christ receives them. . . .*

*Everything
converges in him,
and in his persona
and activity
everything finds
wholeness and meaning.*

Patricia Wilson-Kastner

My God, My God, he cried,
if he is quoted right. . . .
Somehow that moan is comforting
to us, alone at night,
who tremble, daring dawn,
that He, so wise and strong,
should weep and ask for aid.
    Somehow, my lovely distant god,
    it makes me less afraid.

Mirian Kessler

Stephen Frost, *Crucifix with Antlers*

Frost places the antlers of a deer on the image of the crucified Jesus, bringing the fragile, natural world
into solidarity with the death of Jesus.

Georgia O'Keeffe, *Black Cross, New Mexico*

we thank thee god almighty for dying

(forgive us, o life! the sin of Death)

E. E. Cummings

What remains incontestable is the fact that, in spite of what is reported about his curing the sick and raising the dead to life in Galilee and other places, Jesus displayed on the cross nothing but utter helplessness and weakness. Nowhere does the passion narrative depict Jesus except in this utterly powerless image. The reason is that love, in terms of this world's values, is forever vulnerable and helpless. . . . Jesus, powerless on the cross, is the symbol of love—nay, the very incarnation of Love.

Shusaku Endo

Giotto, *The Crucifixion*

Anima Christi (Soul of Christ)

Soul of Christ, sanctify me
Body of Christ, save me
Blood of Christ, inebriate me
Water from the side of Christ,
    wash me
Passion of Christ, strengthen me
O Good Jesus, hear me
Within thy wounds, hide me
Permit me not to be separated
    from Thee
From the wicked foe defend me
At the hour of my death call me
And bid me to come to Thee
That with Thy saints I may
    praise Thee
For ever and ever. Amen

Ignatius of Loyola

We adore you, O Christ,
and we bless you.
Because by your holy cross you have
    redeemed the world.

Traditional prayer of the Good Friday liturgy

Frank Wesley, *Easter Morning*

The reality that the followers encounter

is astonishing, wonderful, even frightening:

God has raised Jesus from the dead! Three women approach the tomb on Easter morning. Jesus' "follow me" has brought them to a journey's end where they anticipate sadness and mourning as they perform the last service of honor to the dead. But instead, life is restored, hope is renewed, the "Way" continues! Christ's disciples share the incredible stories of encountering the risen Jesus: in a locked room, by the lakeshore, on the road to Emmaus. Christ is risen, alleluia!

The resurrection experience transformed the followers of Jesus; stories in Acts tell of the new communities formed in his name, and of the joyful witness by preaching and sharing resources the followers made to the world.

The church continues the Easter proclamation by word and deed, renewing its hope and calling on the power of the risen Christ to overcome sin and death in the world. The church wears white and gold in this festival season of fifty days: Christ is risen indeed. Alleluia!

Easter
Life and hope restored

JESUS IS RISEN!

As they entered the tomb, they saw

a youth, dressed in a white robe,

sitting on the right side; and they were

alarmed. But the youth said to them,

"Do not be alarmed; you are looking

for Jesus of Nazareth, who was crucified.

Jesus has been raised, and the body

is not here. Look, there is the

place they laid the body."

Mark 16:5–6

When we are all despairing;
when the world is full of grief;
when we see no way ahead,
   and hope has gone away:

Roll back the stone.

Although we fear change;
although we are not ready;
although we'd rather weep
   and run away:

Roll back the stone.

Because we're coming with the women;
because we hope where hope is vain;
because you call us from the grave
   and show the way:

Roll back the stone.

Janet Morley

Frank Wesley, *Easter Morning*

God, I am sorry
I ran from you.
I am still running,
running from
that knowledge,
that eye, that love
from which
there is no refuge.
For you meant
only love,
and I felt only fear,
and pain.
So once in Israel
love came
to us incarnate,
stood in the
doorway between
two worlds,
and we were all afraid.

Annie Dillard

José Clemente Orozco, *The White House*

The response of the women at the tomb in Mark's Gospel—to run away frightened—is depicted here. The Resurrection is suggested by the dazzling light reflected on the white building and in the faces of the women hastening away.

But Mark, the harshest, the sparest of the Gospel writers, gives us an unhopeful Easter. Many scholars believe that the manuscript actually ended with a failure of nerve. The women, seeing the angel at the empty tomb, are terrified. The angel tells them to bring the message of Christ's resurrection to the disciples, but they don't. It is believed that the original manuscript ended with this verse: "Then they went out and ran away from the tomb, beside themselves with terror. They said nothing to anybody but they were afraid."

Mary Gordon

Cancion

When I am the sky
a glittering bird
slashes at me with the knives of song.

When I am the sea
fiery clouds plunge into my mirrors,
fracture my smooth breath with crimson sobbing.

When I am the earth
I feel my flesh of rock wearing down:
pebbles, grit, finest dust, nothing.

When I am a woman—O, when I am
a woman,
my wells of salt brim and brim,
poems force the lock of my throat.

Denise Levertov

Levertov's poem gives voice to the fear
of women—like those at the tomb
in Mark's Gospel—who struggle
to speak from their experience.

God of terror and joy,

you arise to shake the earth.

Open our graves and give us back the past;

so that all that has been buried

may be freed and forgiven,

and our lives may return to you

through the risen Christ, Amen.

Janet Morley

Georgia O'Keeffe, *Abstraction—White Rose, III*

Representations of the Resurrection are impossible. O'Keeffe's abstract
painting may suggest what the women experienced: beauty and mystery.

195

OF ONE HEART AND SOUL

Now the whole group of those who believed were of one heart and soul, and no one claimed private ownership of any possession, but everything they owned was held in common. With great power the apostles gave their testimony to the resurrection of the Sovereign Jesus, and great grace was upon them all.

Acts 4:32–33

"There was not a needy person among them." By seeing to it that the needy are cared for, the early church came to embody the Old Testament ideal (cf. Deut. 15:4). Yet by sharing goods in common, they also came to embody the Greek ideal, which held that "for friends all things are common." Clearly, Luke is presenting the early church as the embodiment of both the Jewish and Greek ideal community in which unity and charity thrive.

Fred Craddock

Faith Ringgold, *Church Picnic*, quilt

The quiltmaker and artist Faith Ringgold paints on fabric the story of a 1909 church picnic in Atlanta.

It is the story of a congregation's hope, relationship, and sharing.

We are not alone, we live in God's world.

We believe in God:
    who has created and is creating,
    who has come in Jesus,
    the Word in the flesh,
    to reconcile and make new,
    who works in us and others
    by the Spirit.

We trust in God.

We are called to be the Church:
    to celebrate God's presence,
    to love and serve others,
    to seek justice and resist evil,
    to proclaim Jesus, crucified and risen,
    our judge and our hope.

In life, in death, in life beyond death,
    God is with us.

We are not alone.
Thanks be to God.

United Church of Canada, "A New Creed"

Faith Ringgold, *Church Picnic*, quilt detail

All of my family were God-fearing,

    and I came up in an atmosphere charged with faith,

hope and the Holy Spirit. Outwardly we sang; inwardly we prayed.

From *God Struck Me Dead: Voices of Ex-Slaves*

We have heard about you,
God of all power.
You made the world out of kindness,
creating order out of confusion;
you made each one of us in your own image;
your fingerprint is on every soul.
So we praise you.
We praise and worship you.

We have heard about you,
Jesus Christ:
the carpenter who left his tools and trade;
the poor man who made others rich;
the healer who let himself be wounded;
the criminal on whom the soldiers spat
not knowing they were fouling the face of God;
the savior who died and rose again.
So we praise you.
We praise and worship you.

We have heard about you,
Holy Spirit.
You broke the bonds of every race and nation,
to let God speak in every tongue;
you made the disciples drunk with grace;
you converted souls and emptied pockets;
you showed how love made all things new
and opened the doors to change and freedom.
So we praise you.
We praise and worship you.

Iona Community

Anna Raimondi,
And It Filled All the House

This Hawaiian banner painted on a grass mat
celebrates the gift of God's Spirit
among God's people.

YOU ARE WITNESSES

Then Jesus opened their minds to understand the scriptures, and said to them, "Thus it is written, that the Messiah is to suffer and to rise from the dead on the third day, and that repentance and forgiveness of sins is to be proclaimed in the Messiah's name to all the nations, beginning from Jerusalem. You are witnesses of these things."

Luke 24:45–48

As the risen Jesus appeared to them, "in their joy they were disbelieving" (v. 41).
It is as if they were saying exuberantly, "We just can't believe it. We just can't believe it."
But finally they did believe, and Jesus entrusted them with the task of witnessing to him.

Paul Hammer

Frederick Horsman Varley, *Liberation*

God has been met and known,
even in a human life that
was once a helpless infant.
In a human life the limits
of finitude have been broken,
including the ultimate
barrier of death, that is the
story we have to tell. . . .
[But] we do not capture Christ.
Our minds do not embrace Christ.
Our words point to Christ.
Our images interact with Christ. . . .
Who is Christ for our day?
What images can we employ
that will enable us to be the body
of Christ with integrity while
remaining women and men of
relevance in our generation?

John Shelby Spong

Osmond Watson, *Hallelujah*, detail

Creed from Nicaraguan Mass

Firmly I believe, Lord,
that your prodigious mind
created the whole earth.
To your artist's hand beauty owed its birth:
the stars and the moon,
the cottages, the lakes,
little boats bobbing down river to the sea,
vast coffee plantations,
white cotton fields
and the forests felled by the criminal axe.

In you I believe,
maker of thought and music,
maker of the wind,
maker of peace and love.

Christ the worker, I believe in you,
light of light, God's true
only begotten son,
that to save the world you
in Mary's humble womb grew
and became human.
I believe that you were beaten,
treated with scorn,
martyred on the cross
under Pilate's command.

I believe in you, friend,
human Christ, Christ the worker,
death you've overcome.
Your fearful suffering brought
the new human being
born for freedom.
You still rise again
each time we raise an arm
to defend the people
from profiteering dominion,
because you're alive on the farm,
in the factory, and in school.
I believe your fight goes on,
I believe in your Resurrection.

Haleluya! Pelo tsa rona
Halleluya! We Sing Your Praises

Words and music: South African

Refrain

Ha - le - lu - ya! Pe - lo tsa ro - na, di tha - bi - le ka - o - fe -
Hal - le - lu - ya! We sing your prais - es, all our hearts with glad - ness are

la. Ha - le - lu - ya! Pe - lo tsa ro - na, di tha - bi - le ka - o - fe -
filled. Hal - le - lu - ya! We sing your prais - es, all our hearts with glad - ness are

Last time, end   *Stanzas*

la. 1 Ke Mo - re - na Je - so, ya re du - me - let - seng,
filled. 1 Je - sus Christ said to us: I am wine, I am bread,
2 Christ now sends us all out, strong in faith, free of doubt;

To Refrain

ya re du - me - let - seng, ho tsa - mai - sa e - van - ge - di.
I am wine, I am bread, give to all who hun - ger and thirst.
strong in faith, free of doubt; tell to all the joy - ful Good News.

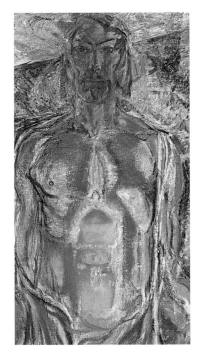

Frederick Horsman Varley,
Liberation, detail

I believe in you, friend, human Christ, death you've overcome.

LET US LOVE

We know love by this, that Jesus laid down life for us—and we ought to lay down our lives for one another. How does God's love abide in anyone who has the world's goods and sees a brother or sister in need and yet refuses help? Little children, let us love, not in word or speech, but in truth and action.

1 John 3:16–18

The meaning of the cross, of redemptive suffering, also appears in a different light for those who suffer and are killed as part of the struggle for justice. Too often Christians have treated the suffering Christ as some kind of cosmic legal transaction with God to pay for the sins of humanity, as though anyone's sufferings and death could actually "pay for" others' sins! Christ's cross is used to inculcate a sense of masochistic guilt, unworthiness and passivity in Christians. . . .

[Thus] to accept and endure evil is regarded as redemptive. . . . Solidarity with the poor and with those who suffer does not mean justifying these evils, but struggling to overcome them. As one struggles against evil, one also risks suffering and becomes vulnerable to retaliation and violence to those who are intent on keeping the present system intact. . . . But risking suffering and even death on behalf of a new society, we also awaken hope.

Rosemary Radford Ruether

Diego Rivera, *The Flower Carrier*

The famous Mexican painter Diego Rivera strangely combines backbreaking toil of workers with colorful and fragrant beauty.

For the People

If I were a bird
and able to fly afar,
I would like to be a white dove
to guide the people to freedom.

If I were a grain of sand,
I would throw myself down
to make a path for the people.

If I were the cloud in the sky,
I would shelter and bring rains
to the rice field.

I would sacrifice my life
for the suffering people.
I would sacrifice my self
no matter how many times
I would have to die.

Anna May Say Pa, Burma Institute of Theology

José Calderon Salazar,
Guatemalan correspondent
of the Mexican newspaper
Excelsior, reported these words
spoken to him over the
telephone by Archbishop
Oscar Romero about two weeks
before his murder.

Michael Tracy, *River Pierce: Sacrifice II*

Michael Tracy's work combines ritual and art, suffering and sacrifices, each permeating life. On Good Friday 1990, Tracy burned his ten-foot-high processional cross in the Rio Grande.

I have often been threatened with death. Nevertheless, as a Christian, I do not believe in death without resurrection. If they kill me, I shall arise in the Salvadoran people. I say so without meaning to boast, with the greatest humility. . . .

Martyrdom is grace of God that I do not believe I deserve. But if God accepts the sacrifice of my life, let my blood be a seed of freedom and the sign that hope will soon be reality. Let my death, if it is accepted by God, be for the liberation of my people and as a witness of hope in the future.

You may say, if they succeed in killing me, that I pardon and bless those who do it. Would that thus they might be convinced that they will waste their time. A bishop will die, but the church of God, which is the people, will never perish.

Archbishop Oscar Romero

Maurice Sendak, *In the Dumps*

Maurice Sendak, a popular writer and illustrator of children's books, has taken a pair of Mother Goose rhymes and turned them into a parable of modern responsibility in the face of homelessness. Under a moon that silently expresses hope for moral action, the homeless children Jack and Guy encounter a child even poorer than they in "the dumps . . . [where] the houses are built without walls." They choose their response: not violence, but sharing of their meager resources, and bring him "home."

Jack and Guy

Went out in the rye

And they found a little boy

With one black eye.

Come says Jack let's knock him

On the head

No says Guy

Let's buy him some bread

You buy one loaf

And I'll buy two

And we'll bring him up

As other folk do.

Traditional rhyme from Mother Goose,
interpreted by Maurice Sendak

We gather to worship, O God,
under the shadow of the cross,
sign of human shame and divine wisdom.
Like Jesus, we would follow faithfully in your way;
like Jesus, we would live to you and die to you.
We are your people;
we belong to you.
We offer you our worship and our lives.
May your name be glorified in your church
as we are open to your presence today;
through Jesus Christ.
Amen.

United Church of Christ Book of Worship

Laughter at Dawn

ABIDE IN ME

Abide in me as I abide in you. Just as the branch cannot bear fruit by itself unless it abides in the vine, neither can you unless you abide in me. I am the vine, you are the branches. Those who abide in me and I in them bear much fruit, because apart from me you can do nothing.

John 15:4–5

. . . the horizon is still quite dark,
but hope is about to dawn.
The seed of salvation is sprouting,
as earth makes ready.
What about the roots of our hearts? . . .

Pierre Talec

Ainslie Roberts, *Laughter at Dawn*

The tree rising in the otherwise barren landscape refracts the sun and roots itself deeply to find sources of water. It makes a home for the birds and shade for the human community.

Robert Lentz, *Tree of Life*

The metaphor of vine and branches represents the unity of Jesus and the disciples. The unity is a given, but it does not exist apart from the disciples' own participation. Jesus is both the one who commands them to abide and bear fruit and the one who enables them to do so. Their bearing of fruit is proof that they are Jesus' disciples. Jesus has linked discipleship with mutual love. . . . The abiding and bearing fruit of which Jesus speaks is the mutuality of love among the disciples.

D. Moody Smith

It is crucial that we be rooted
in someone, if not somewhere.
Pilgrim people on the move
root in relationships.
I am the vine, said Jesus,
extending himself through time and space
to graft us as branch.
To claim that continuity
we must submit to pruning,
sinking ourselves unconditionally
into the will of him in whom
we live and move and are.

Miriam Therese Winter

And from what source,
O tree—
since of yourself you are dead and barren—
do you get these fruits of life?
From the tree of life—
for unless you are engrafted into him
you would have no power
to produce any fruit at all,
because you are nothing.

Catherine of Siena

Tree

Look at me, Lord;
with my arms spread out,
my hands open,
and my heart filled with goodness,
I am like a tree!

And I am even bigger
than the tree there in the wood:
because, Lord, I bear fruit in all seasons,
even in winter, when skies are grey
and cold seizes the earth and its people
in an icy grip.

Look at me, Lord, I am like a tree,
and I say to everyone I meet,
Come and eat the fruit of my tree!
Come and share my smile
if sadness has brought you down!
Come and taste my forgiveness
if malice has enveloped you!
Come and pick my friendship
if fear has seized you!
Come and taste my joy
if misfortune has wounded you!
Come to my tree and help yourself!

Look at me, Lord:
just as you asked,
I am a tree which bears good fruit.

Charles Singer

Kimiyoshi Endo, *Vine and Branches*

So through you who are life
we will produce the fruit of life
if we choose to engraft ourselves into you.

Catherine of Siena

Christ, you are stem, stalk, tree!
Let your fruit take root in me.

Miriam Therese Winter

O sing to God a new song. God has remembered God's steadfast love and faithfulness to the house of Israel. All the ends of the earth have seen the victory of our God.

Psalm 98:1a, 3

SING A NEW SONG

When Mahalia Sings

We used to gather at the high window
of the holiness church and, on tip-toe,
look in and laugh at the dresses, too small
on the ladies, and how wretched they all
looked—an old garage for a church, for pews,
old wooden chairs. It seemed a lame excuse
for a church. Not solemn or grand,
with no real robed choir, but a loose jazz band,
or so it sounded to our mocking ears.
So we responded to their hymns with jeers.

Sometimes those holiness people would dance,
and this we knew sprang from deep ignorance
of how to rightly worship God, who after
all was pleased not by such foolish laughter
but by the stiffly still hands in our church
where we saw no one jump or shout or lurch
or weep. We laughed to hear those holiness
rhythms making a church a song fest:
we heard this music as the road to sin,
down which they traveled toward that end.

I, since then, have heard the gospel singing
of one who says I worship with clapping
hands and my whole body, God, whom we must
thank for all this richness raised from dust.
Seeing her high-thrown head reminded
me of those holiness high-spirited,
who like angels, like saints, worshipped as whole
men with rhythm, with dance, with singing soul.
Since then, I've learned of my familiar God—
He finds no worship alien or odd.

Quandra Prettyman

James Chapin, *Ruby Green Sings*

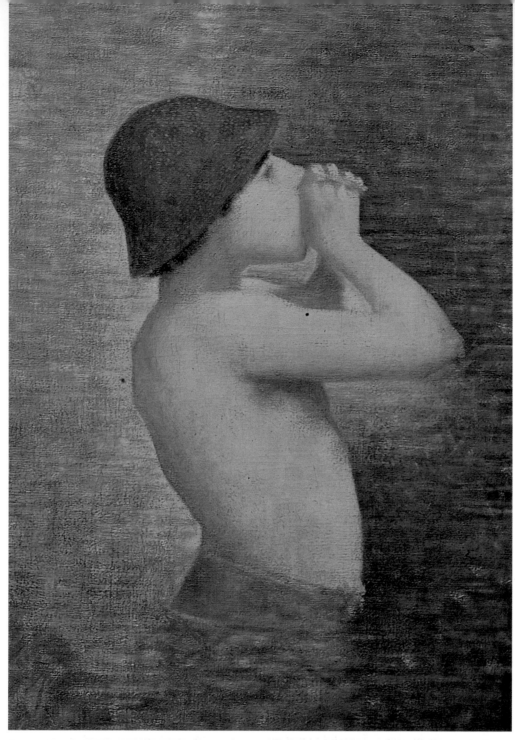

Georges Seurat, *Bathers at Asnières*, detail

After the [leader's] death, his disciples came together and talked about the things he had done. When it was Rabbi Schneur Zalman's turn, he asked them: "Do you know why our master went to the pond every day at dawn and stayed there for a little while before coming home again?" They did not know why. Rabbi Zalman continued: "He was learning the song with which the frogs praise God. It takes a very long time to learn that song."

Martin Buber

Amazing grace! How sweet the sound.

Was blind, but now I see.

John Newton

John Newton (1725–1807) became the captain of a slave ship during the height of the African slave trade. After his conversion he gave up the slave trade and became a minister. He wrote the much beloved song "Amazing Grace." In his journals he wrote: "I was, above most living, a fit person to proclaim that faithful saying, 'That Jesus Christ came into the world to save the chief of sinners.' "

Ma Rainey: The blues help you get out of bed in the morning. You get up knowing you ain't alone. There's something wise in the world. Something's been added by that song. This be an empty world without the blues. I take that emptiness and try to fill it up with something.

August Wilson

Come on Children, Let's Sing

God Almighty has brought us out,
none like God without a doubt.
Come on children, let's sing
'bout the goodness of our God.

Hallelujah!
Come on children, let's sing
'bout the goodness of our God.
Come on children, let's shout
all about God's rich reward.
Guide our footsteps every day,
keeps us in the narrow way.
Come on children, let's sing
'bout the goodness of our God.

African American Traditional Spiritual

T H A T   T H E Y   M A Y   B E   O N E

Jesus said, "I am no longer

in the world, but they are

in the world, and I am coming

to you. Holy God, Father

and Mother, protect them

in your name that you have

given me, so that they may

be one, as we are one."

John 17:11

George Tooker, *Embrace of Peace*

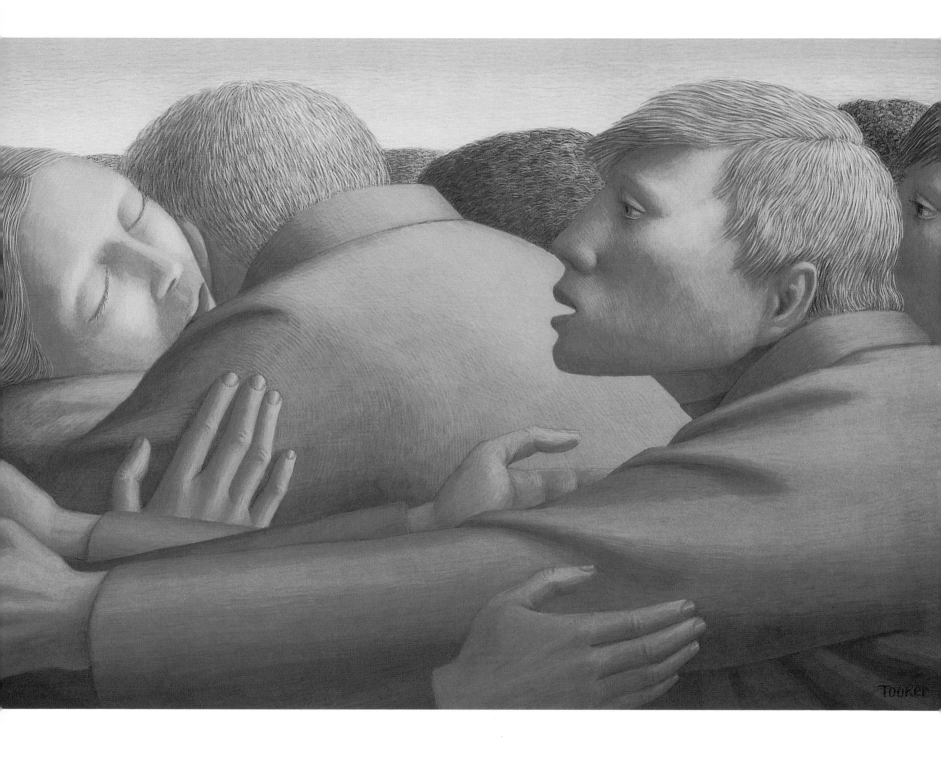

Before sharing the bread and wine, parishioners offer "greetings of peace," turning to each other and to those nearby to exchange a handshake or embrace. For Tooker, the embrace symbolizes the community he has found in the church, and the community he hopes to find in paradise. The painting is thus a visual rendering of heaven and earth where the sexes and races mix harmoniously. It is where "we should be."

Thomas H. Carver

All May Be One, United Church of Christ National Office

[The church] must pray the prayer of Christ together in order to enter most deeply into the shared reality of our new humanity. . . . We are invited to pray together . . . : in the household, among friends, with neighbors or co-workers. The psalms and [New Testament] canticles are our common cry of memory and hope, of promise and pain, of confidence and fear. We are brought together by the human realities they articulate; we can find one another's truth, as well as our own, in their lines. We are urged to pray for one another in their words.

. . . In praying thus together, we take our place with Christ, who intercedes always on our behalf before the throne of God's mercy. Thus is our prayer integral to our mission as church: to open the way for all humanity to make the common journey into the reign of God.

Jennifer Glenn

Living God,
Loving God,
You are the source
of all that is,
and all that is
is holy
when it seeks itself in You.
You are the bond
that unites us all
and erases all division.
May we be one
as You are one in us
and we in You.
Amen.

Miriam Therese Winter

Prayer for Unity in Christ

Lord Jesus,
who on the eve of your death,
prayed that all your disciples
      might be one . . . ,
make us feel intense sorrow
over the infidelity of our disunity.
Give us the honesty to recognize,
and the courage to reject,
whatever indifference towards
      one another,
or mutual distrust, or even enmity,
lie hidden within us.

Enable all of us to meet one
      another in you.
And let your prayer for the unity
      of Christians
be ever in our hearts and on our lips,
unity such as you desire it and by
      the means that you will.

Make us find the way
that leads to unity in you,
who are perfect charity,
through being obedient to the
      Spirit of love and truth. Amen.

Cornerstone Community, Belfast,
Northern Ireland

The Peace Line in East Belfast

Catholic and Protestant homes, only yards apart, are separated by walls known as the "Peace Line," installed in the early 1970s as a way to manage the violence between the two Christian communities. The peace talks of the mid-1990s involve leaders of both traditions in the complex work for justice, peace, and ultimately unity.

The silence is all there is. It is the alpha and the omega. It is God's brooding over the face of the waters; it is the blended note of the ten thousand things, the whine of wings. You take a step in the right direction to pray to this silence, and even to address the prayer to "World." Distinctions blur. Quit your tents. Pray without ceasing.

Annie Dillard

Beauford Delaney, *Can Fire in the Park*

Pentec

The flames of the Spirit burst the confines of the

upper room where the disciples gathered. Fired

by that presence, they went into the wide world.   The festival of Pentecost celebrates the birth of the church. The Holy Spirit came upon the faithful disciples of Jesus to inspire and energize them. They told the story of what God had done for them in Jesus; they preached, they baptized, they healed, they formed communities, they invited the world to join them. The spread of the early church throughout the Mediterranean regions in the generations following Jesus astonished the world.

The season following Pentecost is known in some traditions as "ordinary time," when green signifies the church's continuing work. Discipleship is explored in all its manifestations: to go by faith, not sight; to dance with joy before the presence of God; to test the limits of a sacred boundary and explore the meaning of the Sabbath. The church tells the story, preaching, baptizing, and healing in Jesus' name. We seek to encounter the passionate flames of the Spirit of Christ where they are to be found in the world: sometimes by comfortable hearths, rarely in burning bushes, often on the street around a makeshift fire. We search for the encounter wherever people gather in Jesus' name to seek the warmth and light of a community fostering justice and love. Red is the color given the festival of Pentecost: the red of the Spirit's flames warming, illuminating, fueling the work of the church of Christ in the wide world.

Ost (Cycle B)

Spirit of comfort and power

Spirit of Comfort

The Spirit helps us in our weakness; for we do not know how to pray as we ought, but that very Spirit intercedes with sighs too deep for words. And God, who searches the heart, knows what is the mind of the Spirit, because the Spirit intercedes for the saints according to the will of God.

Romans 8:26–27

Come down, O Love divine,
Seek out this soul of mine
And visit it with Your own ardor glowing;
O Comforter, draw near, Within my heart appear,
And kindle it, Your holy flame bestowing.

Bianco da Siena, translated by Richard Frederick Littledale

Beauford Delaney, *Can Fire in the Park*

Vivid colors thick on canvas convey the need for fire for the homeless in the city. Around the fire is heat, life, comfort, and community.

Betty LaDuke, *Africa: Market Day Dreams*

Soplo de Dios viviente
Breath of the Living God

Soplo de Dios viviente
que en el principio cubriste el agua;
Soplo de Dios viviente
que fecundaste la creación.

¡Ven hoy a nuestras vidas
infúndenos tus dones,
Soplo de Dios viviente,
oh Santo Espíritu Creador!

Breath of the living God,
who in the beginning moved o'er the waters,
Breath of the living God,
by whom all creation was first conceived;

Come now and live within us,
come, let your gifts enrich us,
Breath of the living God,
our Creator Spirit, eternal Source.

Breath of the living God,
whose eternal Word came to dwell among us,
Breath of the living God,
by whom all creation has been renewed;

Come now and live within us,
come, let your gifts enrich us,
Breath of the living God,
our Creator Spirit, eternal Source.

Osvaldo Catena, translated by
The New Century Hymnal

A Litany for Pentecost

When the day of Pentecost had come they were all together in one place and all of the many foreigners heard the witnesses speaking in their own tongue.
Come, Holy Spirit, witness to us also in our several languages.

Speak in the language of our need.
Let us hear how our deepest hungers, desires, and aspirations can be fulfilled by your goodness and in your service.
Come, Holy Spirit, give us that good news again.

Speak in the language of our fear.
Let us hear how our worries about the future, and about each other, and about ourselves, can find rest in your providential care.
Come, Holy Spirit, give us that encouraging news again. . . .

Speak in the language of our gratitude.
Let us hear how our honest thanks relate us, not only to those with whom we live, but also to you, the Lord and Giver of life.
Come, Holy Spirit, give us that enlarging news again. . . .

Speak to us in the language of hope.
Let us hear how our yearning and our expectations are not just wishful thinking, but responses to your promise.
Come, Holy Spirit, give us that good news again. . . .

Models for Ministers I

HOLY, HOLY, HOLY

In the year that King Uzziah died, I saw God sitting on a throne, high and lofty; and the hem of God's robe filled the temple. Seraphs were in attendance above God. And one called to another and said: "Holy, holy, holy is the God of hosts; the whole earth is full of God's glory."

Isaiah 6:1–2a, 3

God is far off, unapproachable, mysterious, uncontrollable; and yet, amazingly, this same unapproachable and mysterious God draws us near and touches us. . . . These two, the beyondness and the nearness, are always held together in tension.

Edmund A. Steimle

O Light!
Divine and one Holy Trinity,
we, born of the earth,
glorify you always
together with the heavenly hosts.
At the raising of the morning light
shine forth upon our souls
your intelligible light.

Matin hymn, Armenian Sunrise Office

Manuscript illumination, *The Vision of Isaiah*, c. 1000

The eleventh-century artist depicts the images in Isaiah's famous vision.

You are a fire, ever burning and never consumed. . . .
You are a light, ever shining and never fading. . . .
You are goodness beyond all goodness, beauty beyond all beauty,
wisdom beyond all wisdom. . . .

Catherine of Siena

Manuscript illumination,
The Vision of Isaiah, c. 1000, detail

In mystery and grandeur
we see the face of God
in earthiness and the ordinary
we know the love of Christ.

In heights and depths
and life and death:
the spirit of God
is moving among us.

Let us praise God.

I will light a light
in the name of God
who lit the world
and breathed the breath of life into me.

I will light a light
in the name of the Son
who saved the world
and stretched out his hand to me.

I will light a light
in the name of the Spirit
who encompasses the world
and blesses my soul with yearning.

We will light three lights
for the trinity of love:
God above us,
God beside us,
God beneath us:
the beginning,
the end,
the everlasting one.

From *In Spirit and in Truth*

How Wonderful the Three-in-One

How wonderful the Three-in-One,
whose energies of dancing light
are undivided, pure and good,
communing love in shared delight.

Before the flow of dawn and dark,
Creation's Lover dreamed of earth,
and with a caring deep and wise,
all things conceived and brought to birth.

The Lover's own Beloved, in time,
between a cradle and a cross,
at home in flesh, gave love and life
to heal our brokenness and loss.

Their Mutual Friend all life sustains
with greening power and loving care,
and calls us, born again by grace,
in Love's communing life to share.

How wonderful the Living God:
Divine Beloved, Empow'ring Friend,
Eternal Lover, Three-in-One,
our hope's beginning, way and end.

Brian Wren

Westminster Abbey

The medieval cathedral represents a breakthrough in gothic architecture: the arches allowed for more height and more light to enter the space through the stained glass windows. The sanctuary, flooded with light, suggests both the splendor and the intimacy of God's presence.

One sabbath Jesus was going

through the grainfields;

and as they made their way

the disciples began to pluck

heads of grain. The Pharisees

said to Jesus, "Look, why

are they doing what is not

lawful on the sabbath?"

Mark 2:23–24

Jesus' authority manifests itself
throughout the first major
section of Mark. Mark 2:15–27
tells stories of a series of controversies
that leave his followers and his
questioners marveling at a paradox:
Jesus seems to defy traditions
about the authority of God, yet acts
with the authority of God.

Ben Shahn, *Beatitude*

Shahn's artistry demonstrates a reversal of the expected. He depicts the wheatfield in its golden abundance, yet the sheaves of wheat are black, not gold! The figure in the midst of the field is reminiscent of Mark's Jesus, who enjoyed the abundance of the wheat even on the Sabbath.

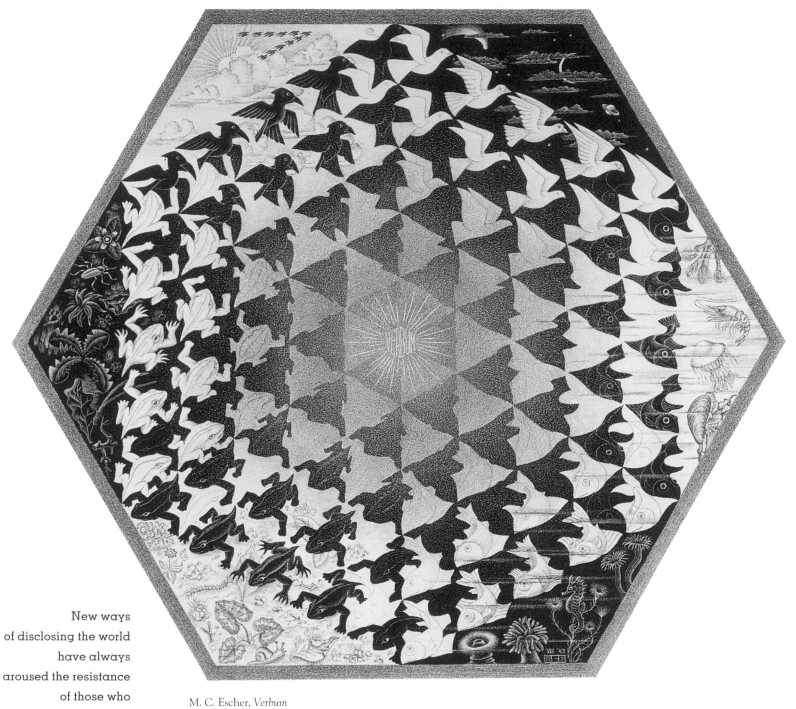

New ways
of disclosing the world
have always
aroused the resistance
of those who
wanted to stay securely
with the familiar.
. . . It is the fate of every
unfamiliar way
of looking at the world.

Paul Tillich

M. C. Escher, *Verbum*

Escher was a master of paradox. His lithograph suggests at once creation of the world, evolution of its creatures, and relationships among elements usually seen in opposition to one another: light and dark, sea and air.

Open our minds and hearts
to the meaning and the cost
of a changing day.

George F. MacLeod

We should not be surprised at the
unexpected quality of the way God counts
and measures, for what little the Bible reveals
to us of the mystery of God's action
indicates that the "new order" means "new math."
In the biblical accounts the liberating
dynamic of God's action often stands out
as a paradox in the midst of the expectations
and social situations of the old order.

Letty M. Russell

Come, Holy Spirit, and show us what is true.
In a world of great wealth
where many go hungry
and fortunes are won and lost
by trading in money,
   Come, Holy spirit, and show us what is true.

In a world of great knowledge
where many die in ignorance
and every piece of information
has a price in the market-place,
   Come, Holy Spirit, and show us what is true.

In a world of easy communication,
where words leap between continents
and we expect to see a picture
to illustrate each item of the news,
   Come, Holy Spirit, and show us what is true.

In a Church which speaks a thousand accents,
divided over doctrine, creed and ministry,
more anxious for itself than for the Gospel,
   Come, Holy Spirit, and show us what is true.

In a Church touched by the flame of Pentecost,
moved to generous sacrifice and costly love,
interpreting the will of God with new insight
   Come, Holy Spirit, and show us what is true.

Stephen Orchard, *United Reformed Church Prayer Handbook*

THE ETERNAL

because we look not at what can be seen but at what cannot be seen; for what can be seen is temporary, but what cannot be seen is eternal. For we know that if the earthly tent we live in is destroyed, we have a building from God, a house not made with hands, eternal in the heavens.

2 Corinthians 4:18–5:1

Our earthly existence is now comparable to that of a tent, the very symbol of transience; for, like a tent, our human existence finally folds. In contrast to the earthly tent of our existence, however, God gives us a "house not made with hands" . . . "eternal in the heavens."

Carl R. Holladay

I often remember a boy
or girl looking, looking
with eager passion, toward
a spiritual horizon that
has escaped my eyes and
maybe everyone else's.
These intensely personal
visionary moments, as
I think of them, sometimes
conveyed softly or tersely,
sometimes rendered with
eloquence and compelling
power, are times when
a mix of psychological
surrender and philo-
sophical transcendence
offers the nearest thing
to Kierkegaard's
"leap of faith" I can
expect to see.

Robert Coles

Lin Xia Jiang, *Parade of Winds, Series I*

Christo and Jeanne-Claude, *Running Fence, Sonoma and Marin Counties, California, 1972–1976*

This art installation, though ironically itself temporary, nevertheless points the way to an understanding of eternity—
it appears to go on forever, to extend out of sight, beyond the horizon, into infinity.

I have recovered it.

Eternity

It is the sea

Matched with the sun.

Arthur Rimbaud

You promise to all who trust you
forgiveness of sins and fullness of grace,
courage in the struggle for justice and peace,
your presence in trial and rejoicing,
and eternal life in your realm which has no end.

Statement of Faith, United Church of Christ

**O God, who broughtst me from the rest of last night
Unto the joyous light of this day,
Be Thou bringing me from the new light of this day
Unto the guiding light of eternity.
Oh! from the light of this day
Unto the guiding light of eternity.**

Celtic prayer, translated by Alexander Carmichael

LIVE BY FAITH

So we are always confident;

for we walk by faith, not by sight.

2 Corinthians 5:6a, 7

*One who walks
by sight will obviously
focus on the visible
and thereby will see only
what is temporary,
whereas the one who walks
by faith will see beyond
the visible to what is
permanent and eternal.
The life of faith, then,
by definition transcends
bodily existence as it draws
its sustaining power
from the risen Lord whom
we know but cannot see,
except with the eyes
of faith.*

Carl Holladay

Caminante, no hay camino.

Se hace camino al andar.

Traveler, there is no road; the way is made by walking.

Antonio Machado

Ethan Hubbard, *Sisters in the Wind*

I walk in emptiness; I hear my breath. . . . I am walking, light as any handful of aurora;
I am light as sails, a pile of colorless stripes; I cry "heaven and earth indistinguishable!"
and the current underfoot carries me and I walk.

Annie Dillard

Ben Shahn, *The Red Stairway*

About fifteen years ago I painted a picture called *The Red Stairway*. It showed a [one-legged] man walking up an endless stair, and then when he came to the top of that stair he came down again. And the whole thing was in the rubble and ruin of a burned out building. To me this is both the hope . . . and the fate of [humanity], you know. It's obvious, almost, that [we] seem . . . to recover from the most frightful wars, the most frightful plagues, and go . . . right on again when [we] know . . . full well that [we're] going into another one: but that's the eternal hope in the human being.

Ben Shahn

I Believe

I believe that there's
Still hope to live,—not merely to exist,
Somewhere in this
Hopeless whirlpool of life
—a hand extended to help.
In these battered days,
You will find, if you search,
—one who has offered to mend.
I know that somewhere,
In this canyon of despair,
—there's a place of relief.
Somewhere, in this
Turmoil of confusion,
—a right path to follow
Within this world
Of make-believe,
—a faithful friend awaits you.
In this polluted time,
We lead—a hope to be made clean.

Lai Leng Woon, a seventeen-year-old girl from Singapore

**To listen—in faith—
to find one's way and
have the feeling that,
under God, one is really
finding it again.**

Dag Hammarskjöld

Thuma Mina

*Lead me, Jesus,
    lead me, Jesus,
Lead me, Jesus,
    lead me now.*

South African traditional song

DAVID AND GOLIATH

ut David said to the Philistine,
"You come to me with sword
and spear and javelin; but I come
to you in the name of the God
of hosts, the God of the armies
of Israel, whom you have defied.
This very day God will deliver
you into my hand."

1 Samuel 17:45–46a

Man of Destiny

As a youth, David was a shepherd.
While his flocks munched grass on the hillside,
David practiced the sheep herders' time-honored
defense against unwelcome intruders: the slingshot.

Little did he realize that this skill would catapult
him into the limelight of Israelite history.
The moment came when Philistine armies
invaded Israel and set up camp for an assault.
A sporting Philistine warrior of monstrous size
issued a pre-battle challenge to duel any Israelite.

Young David, not an Israelite warrior at the time,
figured the odds
and surprised everyone by calling the challenge.

The slow-moving Goliath
was no match
for the agile youth and his deadly sling.
David's shepherding days were over
and his career as a warrior was launched.

With natural battle instincts, and a flashing
personality to match, the young warrior
soon captured the imagination of everyone.

Mark Link

David and Goliath, from León Bible of 1162

I hope that what I am sharing this morning will spark images of how we, unlike David, might tame the mighty giant rather than kill him.

Killing enemies is, after all, a very patriarchal way of handling conflict. . . . Re-imagining of the drama of David and Goliath might present it as a story of taming—of befriending and disarming—the giant.

Carter Heyward

You and I are called to participate in taming giants, in healing and liberating the world around us and within us.

Carter Heyward

If I could talk to each youngster . . .
I would have one message to give them.
I would say, "You are important to the world.
You are needed. Most of all, you can
make a difference in someone else's life.
Begin by doing something that shows you care.
That's where satisfaction in life begins.
And if one day you get a feeling that says
you can change the world, trust that feeling.
Because you make a difference. There is
something important that needs to happen
in the world because of you, and it can
happen if you do it."

During my seventeen years as Referee
of the San Francisco Juvenile Court, I saw
hundreds of young people who refused
to be buried.

Mary Conway Kohler

Gian Lorenzo Bernini, *David*

Bernini depicts determination, strength, and grace in this sculpture, which captures the young David poised to battle Goliath.

No coward soul is mine,

No trembler in the world's storm-tossed sphere;

I see Heaven's glories shine

And Faith equal, arming me from Fear.

Emily Brontë

Martine Barrat, *Young Hopeful at Harlem's Artemio Colon Gym*

Jean Ipoustéguy, *David and Goliath*

The sculptor retells the familiar story as a study in contrasts between the two figures.

for if the eagerness is there, the gift is acceptable according to what one has—not according to what one does not have.

2 Corinthians 8:12

Almsgiving, then, is also a means for positioning myself in the world. I place my money (and thus myself, for money is a symbol, albeit not the only one, of my power) in service to what stands above or below me, depending on whether and how I save it or spend it. . . . Here lies a deep truth about the sacred circulation of money, be it almsgiving or tithing: The issue is not obligation but responsibility, not enforcement but valuation. . . . Tithing and its corollaries can perhaps be best understood as weighing of values, an attempt to find one's place in the cosmic network; it is also a measure against which one strives, against which one balances the other demands of life—paying the rent, financing the car, going on vacation.

Philip Zaleski

Stephen Shames, *Mother Clara Hale at Age 87*

Clara McBride Hale's long career caring for sick children began in 1969 when a young woman appeared at her door with a drug-addicted baby.
Before her death at age 87 in 1992, Mother Hale was a foster-care mother for more than four decades. She also founded Hale House, a safe,
loving environment that has nurtured more than 1,000 young victims of New York City's drug and AIDS epidemics.

**Remember that [God] will in [God's] own way and . . . own time complete what we so poorly attempt. Often we do
not achieve for others the good we intend; but we achieve something, something that goes on from our effort. Good
is an overflow. Where we generously and sincerely intend it, we are engaged in a work of creation.**

Iris Murdoch

Carol Fabricatore

God's Love We Deliver is a not-for-profit volunteer organization founded in New York City to provide free meals for home-bound people with AIDS.

God, the multiplier
of gifts, invests
grace in the enterprise
of the gospel and
receives it back again
in the form of ever-
growing thanksgivings.
Or, to translate this
circular flow more
directly . . . : the worldwide hospitality of
believers, one to another,
expands their ability
to welcome God
with their praises.
The new humanity matures,
and God reaps benefits.

John Koenig

Cease to do evil. Learn to do good, search for justice, help the oppressed, be just to the orphan, plead for the widow.

Isaiah 16–17

God's Love, We Deliver Logo

Pablo Picasso, *La Soupe*

The bowl has the look of waiting. When it is empty, waiting is its perfection, for the bowl was made to hold that which cannot hold itself. The bowl is a hand, cupped upward toward the rain. Falling, the rain has nowhere to go and, so, cannot be detained save by supplication. All bowls imitate human hand gesture, palm concave and stretched toward a generosity of heaven. A hand so gestured does not wait *for* anything. Its shape and time *is* waiting. So too with the bowl. The bowl is for praying.

When full, the bowl is still for waiting. Brimming with rain after the passing shower, the bowl is there to catch sun and magnify its exuberance. For jay, thrush, sparrow, the bowl waits on their thirst. It exemplifies the law of service. One thing serves another that serves a third that, in the round-robin exchange, supports the first.

David Applebaum

Ceremony for Completing a Poetry Reading
(Excerpt)

This is a give-away poem
You have come gathering
You have made a circle with me . . .
Within this basket is something
    you have been looking for
all of your life
Come take it
Take as much as you want
I give you seeds of a new way . . .
Come
this is a give-away poem
I cannot go home
until you have taken everything
and the basket which held it

When my hands are empty
I will be full

Chrystos

249

Sent by Jesus

Jesus called the twelve and began to send them out two by two, and gave them authority over the unclean spirits. Jesus ordered them to take nothing for their journey except a staff.

Mark 6:7–8a

The work of Jesus is to continue, and for that purpose the church is called and sent. For that work Jesus grants the word and the power that characterized his own ministry. The church is to go trusting this to be true, never contradicting that trust with the excess baggage of security and wealth that offer the world the image of unbelief. There will be rejection and refusal to listen, to be sure, but there will also be those who will welcome both the ministry and the minister.

Fred Craddock

He is the Way.
Follow Him through the land of Unlikeness,
You will see rare beasts, and have unique adventures.

He is the Truth.
Seek Him in the Kingdom of Anxiety;
You will come to a great city that has expected your return
      for years.

He is the Life!
Love Him in the World of the Flesh;
And at your marriage all its occasions shall dance for joy.

W. H. Auden

Shin Young-Hun, *Outreach of the New Covenant*

Those who set out to share the good news often discover that they are changed in the process. Good news does not always travel on a one-way street.

We not only invite others to join us, but we also respond to the invitation to join others, to learn what they have seen and heard of God's ways and God's word. We join each other. We join together in an unfolding journey of discovery and discipleship.

Martin B. Copenhaver

Thuma Mina
Send Me Now

Thuma mina, thuma mina.
Thuma mina, Somandla.

Seng'ya vuma, Seng'ya vuma,
Seng'ya vuma, Somandla.

Send me, God, send me, God,
Send me, God, send me now.

Lead me, Jesus, lead me, Jesus,
Lead me, Jesus, lead me now.

South African traditional song

Go forth into the world

in peace;

be of good courage;

hold fast to that

which is good;

render to no one evil for evil;

strengthen the fainthearted;

support the weak;

help the afflicted;

honor all people;

love and serve God,

rejoicing in the power

of the Holy Spirit.

Amen.

United Church of Christ

Henry O. Tanner, *Disciples Healing the Sick*

DANCE BEFORE GOD

David and all the house of Israel were dancing before God with all their might, with songs and lyres and harps and tambourines and castanets and cymbals.

2 Samuel 6:5

I cannot dance, O Lord,
Unless You lead me.
If You wish me to leap joyfully,
Let me see You dance and sing—

Then I will leap into Love—
And from Love into Knowledge,
And from Knowledge into the Harvest,
That sweetest fruit beyond human sense.

There I will stay with You, whirling.

Mechtild of Magdeburg

Jan DeBray, *David Dances before the Ark of the Covenant*

Jonathan Green, *The Shout*

I cannot dance,
O God, unless
you lead me.

Film still from *Footloose*

Richmond Barthé, *Exodus Dance*

Barthé depicts the Hebrews dancing for joy
at their liberation from Pharaoh.

The 1984 film *Footloose* tells the story of a teenage boy, Ren MacCormack, and his struggle to bring dance back to a sorrowing small town. In the following scene, Ren defends the senior class dream to have a prom. He shows courage as he challenges the town council's law against dance.

"You see, from the olden times, people danced for a number of reasons—they danced in prayer, or so their crops would be plentiful, or so the hunt would be good." Ren had started pacing back and forth in front of the council members' table. . . .

"People danced to stay physically fit, to show their community spirit. . . . And they danced to celebrate. And that—" He slapped one hand against the other. "—that's the dancing we're talking about. . . .

"Dancing is celebration!" His voice carried to the rafters of the draughty old room. "It cleans out the body and the spirit, and energy that might be destructive suddenly becomes an expression of joy and happiness. For what? Well, for just about everything. For the fact that spring is here, okay? . . .

"Or maybe because we're graduating. And aren't we told . . ." He waited a beat before dropping his first bomb. "Aren't we told in Psalm 149 . . ." He snatched up the Bible. "'Praise ye the Lord. Sing unto the Lord a new song. . . . Let them praise his name *in the dance.*' . . .

"And there was King David—King David—in the book of Samuel. And what did he *do*? 'And David danced before the Lord with all his might . . . leaping and dancing before the Lord.' *Leaping and dancing,* in front of God! . . .

"In Ecclesiastes, we are told, 'There is a time to every purpose under the heaven. . . . A time to weep, and a time to laugh; a time to mourn, and a time to dance.'"

"And there was a time for this law," said [a member of the town council].

Ren turned and, his eyes bright, met the challenge head on. "But not anymore! That time is gone. This is *our* time to dance. This is our way of participating in a rebirth. A new life. . . .

"That's the way it was in the beginning, the way it's always been and that's the way it should be, now and *forever* and *ever.*"

Footloose

Fount of all life, dancing in bliss,
Breaking down walls, making new spaces

Burning up evil, creating afresh,
Calling your people, follow in faith.

Living with Jesus, power in his Name,
Healing the broken, restoring the lame.

…

Seeking the lost, sharing all pain,
Loving at such cost, rising again.

Lighting our path, dancing ahead,
Leading through death, lifting to life.

United Theological College, Bangalore, India

Alan Levenson, *Fancy Dancing*

Fancy dancing is a tradition shared among many Native American communities.
Costumes and choreography are designed primarily for entertainment and pleasure,
improvising from a wide range of traditions.

I will stay with you, whirling!

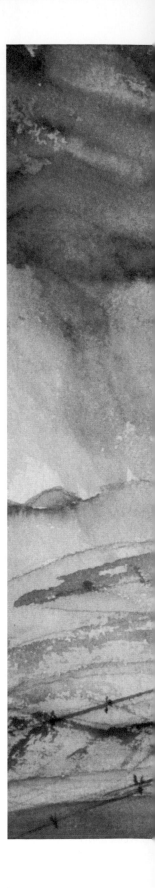

IN ONE BODY

Christ has abolished the law with its commandments

and ordinances, in order to create in Christ one

new humanity instead of two, thus making peace,

and in order to reconcile both groups to God

in one body through the cross.

Ephesians 2:15–16a

The Holy Spirit calls us toward an all-inclusive attitude, a theology
of the wind, a relationship to God and the world that does not try to make
things easy by ruling out whole areas of human experience and whole groups
of human beings. When one goes out to fish, one does not dictate to God
what may or may not be attracted to the bait.

Virginia Ramey Mollenkott

Estelle Ishigo, *Boys with Kite*

The artist of this painting and its subjects, the two little boys, were all interned in the Japanese-American internment camps set up by the United States government during World War II. The boys seem unconcerned about the barbed wire barrier between them and freedom; they find a way over and through it to fly their kite, a traditional symbol of freedom.

the need for one another

Resting in Peace

There is a cemetery—
or perhaps two—
deep in the city
at the intersection of
Narragansett and Montrose Avenues.

It is located, undeniably,
on one piece of ground
but with two entrances,
two names,
two accents,
separated by one fence.

In the north,
Children of the Cross
with names like
Anderson . . . Olsen . . .
Arthur and Anna Christensen . . .
rest forever.
They call their home
Mount Olive.

In the south,
Children of the Menorah
with names like
Rosenberg . . . Weiss . . .
Rebecca and Abraham Goldstein . . .
wait in silence.
They call their home
Mount Mayriv.

The fence—
a strong, high fence with
three strands of barbed wire on top—
separates the graves of
Israel Weinstein
and
Harold Hanson.

I can't help but
wonder
if that fence
is the same barrier
for the dead
as it is
for the living
and
if we couldn't
get by with
just taking it down.

Mark Milligan

It is often when a community is on the verge of breaking up that people agree to talk to each other and look each other in the eye. This is because they realize that it is a question of life or death, that everything will collapse if they do not do something decisive and radically different. Often we have to come to the edge of the precipice before we reach the moment of truth and recognize our own poverty and need of each other, and cry to God for help.

Jean Vanier

Grandfather,
Look at our brokenness.

We know that in all creation
Only the human family
Has strayed from the Sacred Way.

We know that we are the ones
Who are divided
And we are the ones
Who must come back together
To walk the sacred Way.

Grandfather,
Sacred One,
Teach us love, compassion and honor
That we may heal the earth
And heal each other.

Ojibway Prayer

The Wall Came Tumbling Down

An East German border guard peers through a newly created hole in the once impregnable wall.

FIVE THOUSAND FED

One of Jesus' disciples, Andrew, Simon Peter's brother, said to him, "There is a boy here who has five barley loaves and two fish. But what are they among so many people?" Then Jesus took the loaves, and when he had given thanks, he distributed them to those who were seated; so also the fish, as much as they wanted.

John 6:8–9, 11

One Small Boy

The report
on the miracle
of the bread and the fish
is about what happened
to somebody
who gave all he had.
It is, of course, a story about Jesus
multiplying all that bread and that fish.
But
whose bread did he multiply?
Whose fish did he divide?
    It all started
    with the real hero
    of that story:
    one small boy.

                    . . .

    I think that Jesus
    praised that small boy
    who had given all he had. . . .
When you are asked for something
    you think you are unable to give,
    think of that small boy
    of this story,
    and think of the twelve baskets
    full of food given to him
    because he gave
    all he had.

Joseph P. Donders

Alemayehu Bizuneh, *Scene X of the Misereor "Hunger Cloth" from Ethiopia*

The Ethiopian artist Alemayehu Bizuneh paints biblical stories with the brilliant colors of medieval artists.
Painted on a "hunger cloth," this panel disturbs and offers hope.

Jacopo Bassano, *The Feeding of the Five Thousand*

The table fellowship of Christians implies obligation. It is our daily bread that we eat, not my own. We share our bread. Thus we are firmly bound to one another not only in the Spirit but in our whole physical being. The one bread that is given to our fellowship links us together in a firm covenant. Now none dares go hungry as long as another has bread, and anyone who breaks this fellowship of the physical life also breaks the fellowship of the Spirit.

Dietrich Bonhoeffer

I had been hungry, all the Years—
My Noon had Come—to dine—
I trembling drew the Table near—
And touched the Curious Wine—

'Twas this on Tables I had seen—
When turning, hungry, Home
I looked in Windows, for the Wealth
I could not hope—for Mine—

I did not know the ample Bread—
'Twas so unlike the Crumb
The Birds and I, had often shared
In Nature's—Dining Room—

The Plenty hurt me—'twas so new—
Myself felt ill—and odd—
As Berry—of a Mountain Bush—
Transplanted—to the Road—

Nor was I hungry—so I found
That Hunger—was a way
Of Persons outside Windows—
The Entering—takes away—

Emily Dickinson

The decision to feed the world is the real decision.

Adrienne Rich

Eucharistic Loaves and Fish, c. 3rd century, catacomb of San Callisto, Crypt of Lucina, Rome

This depiction in the ancient burial chamber of San Callisto is among the earliest Christian paintings. Decorating crypts in the style of pagan tombs, this painter introduced the most basic Christian symbols.

But speaking the truth in love,

we must grow up in every way into the

one who is the head, into Christ.

Ephesians 4:15

The seed of God
is in us.
If you are an
intelligent
and hard-working
farmer,
it will thrive
and grow
up into God,
whose seed it is,
and its fruits
will be God-fruits,
pear seeds
grow into pear trees,
nut seeds
grow into nut tress,
and God seeds
grow into God.

Meister Eckhart

Jyoti Sahi (India), *Jesus Christ—The Life of the World*

Rembrandt Harmensz van Rijn, *The Apostle Paul in Prison*

Tradition has taught that Paul, exercising his ministry in prison, wrote the letter to the Ephesians (Ephesians 4:1).

Love at the heart of growth

Ephesians 4:1–16 concentrates heavily on the Church. . . . The Church is the sphere into which the readers have entered through their faith and their baptism, the context into which they live out their calling. The major image for this concern . . . is that of the body. . . . The Church is also the fullness of Christ . . . and in its final state can be seen as "the mature person." All this is part of a dynamic picture of a corporate entity which grows as its individual members are involved in a continual process of mutual adjustment and which is on the move toward unity, completeness, maturity and conformity to Christ. . . . The essential ingredient for the achievement of the harmony of unity in diversity is love. Love is the energizing power behind the community's drive to maintain unity, at the heart of its process of truth and all the way through its process of corporate growth.

Andrew T. Lincoln

God . . . is not far away from us,
altogether apart from the world we touch,
hear, smell and taste about us.
Rather [God] awaits us every instant in our action,
in the work of the moment.
There is a sense in which [God]
is at the tip of my pen, my spade, my brush, my needle—
of my heart and of my thought.

Teilhard de Chardin

Leader: Affirmation of ministry is the act
whereby a local church . . .
recognizes the diverse gifts of its members
and celebrates the particular ministry
of each person in the life of the church
or in various settings in the life of the world.

There are different kinds of spiritual gifts,
but the same Spirit gives them.

**People: There are different ways of serving,
but the same God is served.**

Leader: There are different abilities to perform service,
but the same God gives ability to each of us
for our particular service.

**People: The Spirit's presence is shown in some way
in each person for the good of all. . . .**

**People: All of us are Christ's body,
and each one is a part of it.**

United Church of Christ Book of Worship

TOUCH OF AN ANGEL

hen Elijah lay down under the broom tree and fell asleep.

Suddenly an angel touched him and said to him, "Get up

and eat." He looked, and there at his head was a cake

baked on hot stones, and a jar of water.

1 Kings 19:5–6a

If the angel deigns to come, it will be because you
have convinced her, not by your tears, but by your
resolve to make a beginning, to be a beginner.

Rainer Maria Rilke

Dieric Bouts, Elijah and the Angel

Here [Elijah] who was strong has become weak. He cowers before his new enemy, Jezebel. Far from performing another mighty work, he flees into the desert, abandoning life itself.

. . . Under the broom tree in the Negeb {outside of Yahweh's land} Elijah prays Yahweh to take his life, for all that he has lived for—his prophetic ministry and Yahweh's people—are gone. It is there that God takes over, feeding him with angelic food and bringing him in forty days to the Mountain of God . . .

Simon J. DeVries

"It still all comes down to the same thing: life is beautiful. And I believe in God."

Etty Hillesum

This morning I said to Jopie, "It still all comes down to the same thing: life is beautiful. And I believe in God. And I want to be there right in the thick of what people call 'horror' and still be able to say: 'life is beautiful.' And now here I lie in some corner, dizzy and feverish and unable to do a thing. When I woke up just now I was parched, reached for my glass of water, and, grateful for that one sip, thought to myself, 'If I could only be there to give some of those packed thousands just one sip of water.'"

. . . I am with the hungry, with the ill-treated and the dying, every day, but I am also with the jasmine and with that piece of sky beyond my window; there is room for everything in a single life. For belief in God and for a miserable end.

Etty Hillesum

Etty Hillesum, a Dutch Jewish woman living in Holland during the Nazi occupation of the late 1930s to early 1940s, kept a journal of her struggles to survive physically and spiritually.

Entering Rest

Dear Companion of my day,
You are the Holy Mystery I surrender to
when I close my eyes. I give You myself:
the flaws, the mistakes, the petty
self-congratulations. I give You my dear ones:
my fondest hopes for them, my worries,
and my dark thoughts regarding them.
Take my well-constructed separation from me.
Hold me in Your truth.

This day is already past. I surrender it.
When I think about tomorrow, I surrender it, too.
Keep me this night. With You
and in You I can trust not knowing anything.
I can trust incompleteness as a way.
Dark with the darkness, silent with the silence,
help me dare to be that empty one—futureless,
desireless—who breathes Your name even in sleep.

Gunilla Norris

Tadao Tanaka, *Elijah and the Crow*

I am here, Lord.

I don't need to be alone
   at the top of a tree
to talk to you.

Just help me
to be quiet within myself,
so that, like Elijah,
I can listen for you.

Although you do not come
in a great noise,
I can hear you
and you can hear me.

Spirit of God, in me,
help me to pray
in the way best for me.

Joan M. Burns

273

SEEKING GOD'S PURPOSE

Solomon prayed, "Give your servant therefore an understanding mind to govern your people, able to discern between good and evil; for who can govern this your great people?"

1 Kings 3:9

My mother prayed
on her knees at midday,
at night, and first thing
in the morning. Every day
opened up to her to have
God's will done in it.
Every night she totted
up what she'd done
and said and thought,
to see how it squared
with Him. That kind of life
is dreary, people think,
but they're missing the point.
For one thing, such a life
can never be boring.
And nothing can happen
to you that you can't
make use of. Even if you're
racked by troubles,
and sick and poor and ugly,
you've got your soul
to carry through life like
a treasure on a platter.
Going upstairs to pray after
the noon meal, my mother
would be full of energy and
expectation, seriously smiling.

Alice Munro

Jeffery Allan Salter, *Taurian Osborne Prays*
at the New Fellowship Missionary Baptist Church

Judgment of Solomon, seventeenth-century lace

The anonymous lacemaker employing an exquisite array of patterned stitches captured the drama of the story at the moment of Solomon's order to divide the child in half: the soldier poised with the sword raised, the baby naked and defenseless, the women responding. The lacemaker offers clues to the identities of the two women by depicting them in different costumes and postures.

The *Kebra Nagast*, an ancient Abyssinian chronicle, tells of the meeting between the Queen of Sheba and King Solomon. The queen traveled to Israel to test the wisdom of Solomon; satisfied, she became a believer in the One God.

Wisdom is
sweeter than honey,
brings more joy
than wine,
illumines
more than the sun,
is more precious
than jewels.
She causes
the ears to hear
and the heart to comprehend.

I love her
like a mother,
and she embraces me
as her own child.
I will follow
her footprints
and she will not cast me away.

Makeda, Queen of Sheba
(c. 1000 B.C.E.)

Discernment is not logically derived. (Of course, the functions of the mind have a rightful place as part of our personhood! This is not at all to say that one ceases to think rationally and well. It is to say, however, that logic is not the judge of whether a discernment is of God or not. The mind becomes informed by the spirit, rather than the other way around.) Discernment cannot be empirically judged; it is ultimately a faith statement. It is a gamble of faith. It is obedience to an inward monitor—and upon that we risk all. . . . Discernment, far from keeping us "safe," puts us at the outposts of our comfort zones. We choose to live into the fullness of our Light—regardless of the consequences. With Job we echo, "Even though he slay me, yet will I trust that it is God at work in me."

Alastair Heron

The text begins with the initials A. M. D. G. standing for *Ad Maiorem Dei Gloriam*—For the Greater Glory of God—the goal of the exercises. *The Spiritual Exercises of St. Ignatius* has become a classic of Christian spirituality since its first publication in 1548. Developed first by Ignatius Loyola for his early companions in the Society of Jesus, the exercises describe in detail a process for revealing God's way and wisdom.

Jusepe de Ribera, *Ignatius Begins the Spiritual Exercises*

God, give your servant wisdom.

THE DWELLING PLACE

Then Solomon stood before the altar
of God in the presence of all the assembly
of Israel, and spread out his hands
to heaven: "Hear the plea of your servant
and of your people Israel when they
pray toward this place; O hear in heaven
your dwelling place; heed and forgive."

1 Kings 8:22, 30

Psalm 84

Lord, how beautiful you are;
    how radiant the places you dwell in.
My soul yearns for your presence;
    my whole body longs for your light.
Even the wren finds a house
    and the sparrow a nest for herself.
Take me home, Lord; guide me
    to the place of perfect repose.
Let me feel you always within me;
    open my eyes to your love.

Stephen Mitchell

Against the backdrop of non-Israelite religions whose temples housed images of the gods and were thought to be the residences of those gods, ancient Israel affirms that Yahweh does not live in Solomon's temple. Rather, Solomon prays that the ancient promise be fulfilled—that the Lord will choose to allow [God's] name to dwell in the temple. Thus the temple is a place where that name can be called in prayer, and the Lord will hear the prayer.

John H. Hayes

Henri Matisse, *Chapel of the Rosary at Vence, France*

Irish Tourist Board, *Monastery on Skellig Michael*

Monks of the ancient Celtic church dwelt as close to the elements as possible, creating shelters that seemed to extend the rocky islands and cliffs where they lived.

Fouquet, *Construction of the Temple of Jerusalem Under the Order of Solomon*

Solomon's temple is imagined in the most beautiful and grand terms possible by this medieval artist: a great cathedral.

Alyosha did not step on the steps, but went down rapidly. His soul, overflowing with rapture, was craving for freedom and unlimited space. The vault of heaven, studded with softly shining stars, stretched wide and vast over him. From the zenith to the horizon the Milky Way stretched its two arms dimly across the sky. The fresh, motionless, still night enfolded the earth. The white tower and golden domes of the cathedral gleamed against the sapphire sky. . . . The silence of the earth seemed to merge into the silence of the heavens, the mystery of the earth came in contact with the mystery of the stars. . . . Alyosha stood, gazed, and suddenly he threw himself down flat upon the earth.

He did not know why he was embracing it. He could not have explained to himself why he longed so irresistibly to kiss it, to kiss it all, but he kissed it, weeping, sobbing and drenching it with his tears, and vowed frenziedly to love it, to love it for ever and ever. Water the earth with the tears of your gladness and love those tears, it ran in his soul. What was he weeping over? Oh, he was weeping in his rapture even over those stars which were shining for him from the abyss of space and he was not ashamed of that ecstasy. It was as though the threads from all those innumerable worlds of God met all at once in his soul, and it was trembling all over as it came in contact with other worlds.

Fyodor Dostoyevsky

Blessing of a Home

Leader:

In the name of God, peace to this house/place.
God make it a haven for all who live here.
"Behold I stand at the door and knock," says the Lord.
   If you hear my voice and open the door, I will come
   in and eat with you and you with me" (Revelation 3:20).

Householders then say:

Welcome to this/our home.
Blessed be God who dwells in love.
Blessed be God who gives peace and shelter.
Amen.

Leader:

God of hearth and home, maker of love and laughter,
make this a place for reflection and restoration, rest and renewal,
a place where the life of [Name] (and [Name]) may find its strength.

The Lord watch over your going out and your coming in
from this time forward for evermore.

[Name], God bless you and keep you secure in this place.
May your family/companion(s) find
in you Christ's love and understanding.

Hear God's word of benediction:
the fruit of righteousness will be peace
and the result of righteousness,
tranquility and trust for ever,
my people will abide
in secure dwellings
and in quiet resting places.

And now the eternal Spirit,
enfold this home with love;
indwell this home with joy;
and build this home in peace
evermore and evermore.
Amen.

A New Zealand Prayer Book

DOERS OF THE WORD

But be doers of the word,

and not merely hearers

who deceive themselves.

James 1:22

Let every word
be the fruit
of action and reflection.
Reflection alone
without action
or tending toward it
is mere theory,
adding its weight
when we are
overloaded
with it already.
Action alone
without reflection
is being busy
pointlessly.
Honor the Word eternal
and speak
to make
a new world possible.

Helder Camara

Elijah Pierce, *Obey God and Live*

Elijah Pierce—barber, woodcarver, and lay minister—illustrates God's call to read and to live the Holy Bible.

Alleluia
Speak, Jesus, Word of God.
It's your turn to speak. Alleluia.
Alleluia
Brother, who speaks truth to his brothers and sisters,
give us your new freedom.
Free from profit and from fear,
we will live in gospel;
we will shout in gospel: Alleluia.
Alleluia
No power will silence us. Alleluia.
Alleluia
Against the orders of hate
you bring us the law of love.
In the face of so many lies
you are the truth out loud.
Amid so much news of death
you have the word of life.
After so many false promises, frustrated hopes,
you have, Lord Jesus, the last word,
and we have put all our trust in you. Alleluia.
Alleluia
Your truth will set us free. Alleluia.
Alleluia

Pedro Casaldaliga, Brazil

Rick Reinhard, *Base Communities*

Access to words (literacy programs founded on the model of Paulo Freire, Brazilian educator) and to the Word (in the reflection/action processes of Base Christian Communities) laid the foundation for faithful action for change on the part of oppressed peoples in Latin America.

**Human existence cannot be silent,
nor can it be nourished by false words,
but only true words, with which men
and women transform the world.
To exist, humanly, is to name the world,
to change it. . . . Human beings are not
built in silence, but in word, in work,
in action-reflection.**

Paulo Freire

Lord, I keep so busy praising my Jesus,
Keep so busy praising my Jesus,
Keep so busy praising my Jesus,
Ain't got time to die.
'Cause when I'm healing the sick,
I'm praising my Jesus.
Yes I'm praising my Jesus when I'm healing the sick.
Lord, I ain't got time to die.

Lord, I keep so busy working for the kingdom,
Keep so busy working for the kingdom,
Keep so busy working for the kingdom,
Ain't got time to die.
'Cause when I'm feeding the poor,
I'm working for the kingdom.
Yes, I'm working when I'm feeding the poor.
Lord, I ain't got time to die.

'Cause it takes all my time to praise my Jesus,
All of my time to praise my Lord.
If I don't praise him, the rocks gonna cry out,
"Glory and honor, glory and honor!"
Ain't got time to die.

Hall Johnson

Alan S. Weiner/NYT Pictures, *Oseola McCarty*

Working as a washer-woman, Oseola McCarty saved $150,000. She spent little money on herself, binding her ragged Bible to keep Corinthians from falling out. In 1995 she gave the money as a scholarship to the University of Southern Mississippi to share her wealth "with the children."

Text Sources

Foreword

Richard Kearney, *The Wake of Imagination: Toward a Postmodern Culture* (Minneapolis: University of Minnesota Press, 1988), 390.

Tennessee Williams, *A Streetcar Named Desire*, in *The Theatre of Tennessee Williams*, vol. 1 (New York: New Directions Publishing Corporation, 1971), 356.

That We May See: An Introduction

Abraham Joshua Heschel, *The Prophets*, vol. 1 (1955; New York: Harper and Row, 1962), xi.

Proper 17

Nikos Kazantzakis, *The Saviors of God: Spiritual Exercises* (New York: Simon and Schuster, 1960), 128.

Lame Deer and Richard Erdoes, *Lame Deer: Seeker of Visions* (New York: Simon and Schuster, 1972), 115.

Catherine of Siena, *The Dialogue*, trans. Suzanne Noffke (New York: Paulist Press, 1980). Used by permission.

Rabbi Adin Steinsaltz, "The Command Is to Hear," in *Parabola* 19, no. 1 (February 1994), 33.

James Lawson, "Squander Not the Grace of God," in *Sojourners*, July 1992, 14–15. Used by permission.

"Thuma Mina (Send Me Now)," in *The New Century Hymnal* (Cleveland, Ohio: The Pilgrim Press, 1995), no. 360. Copyright © 1984 by Walton Music Corporation. Used by permission.

Robert Frost, "Sitting by a Bush in Broad Daylight," in *The Poetry of Robert Frost* (New York: Henry Holt and Company, 1962). Copyright 1956 by Robert Frost. Copyright 1928, © 1969 by Henry Holt and Co., Inc. Used by permission of Henry Holt and Co., Inc.

Proper 18

E. M. Broner and Naomi Nimrod, "The Women's Haggadah," in *The Telling* (San Francisco: HarperCollins Publishers, 1993), 76, 193. Used by permission of HarperCollins Publishers, Inc.

A Passover Haggadah as Commented Upon by Elie Wiesel, ed. Marion Wiesel (New York: Simon and Schuster, 1993), 24–25.

"Adir Hu (God of Might)," in Howard I. Bogot and Robert J. Orkand, *A Children's Haggadah* (New York: Central Conference of American Rabbis, 1994), 70. Used by permission.

Proper 19

A. M. Klein, "And in That Drowning Instant," in *Voices within the Ark: The Modern Jewish Poets*, ed. Howard Schwartz and Anthony Rudolf (New York: Avon Books, 1980), 758–59. Copyright © McGraw-Hill Ryerson, 1974. Used by permission.

Maya Angelou, *All God's Children Need Traveling Shoes* (New York: Random House, 1986), 207.

Sylvia G. Dunstan, "Crashing Waters at Creation," in *The New Century Hymnal* (Cleveland, Ohio: The Pilgrim Press, 1995), no. 326. Copyright © 1991 by G.I.A. Publications, Inc., Chicago, IL. All rights reserved. Used by permission.

Hal Hopson, *Moses and the Freedom Fanatics* (Dallas: Choristers Guild, 1979), 43. Used by permission.

Proper 20

David Applebaum, *Everyday Spirits* (New York: SUNY, 1993), 131.

Benjamin Chavis, Jr., "Psalm 149," in *Psalms from Prison* (Cleveland, Ohio: The Pilgrim Press, 1994), 54. Used by permission.

Edina, age 12, in *I Dream of Peace: Images of War by Children of Former Yugoslavia* (New York: HarperCollins Publishers, 1994), 47. © 1994 UNICEF. Used by permission of HarperCollins Publishers, Inc.

Janet Schaffran, "Eucharistic Prayer," adapted from *The Didache*, in Janet Schaffran and Pat Kozak, *More than Words: Prayer and Ritual for Inclusive Communities* (Oak Park, Ill.: Meyer-Stone Books, 1988), 51. First edition © 1986 by Pat Kozak, CSJ, and Janet Schaffran, CDP; second revised edition © 1988 by Pat Kozak, CSJ, and Janet Schaffran, CDP. All rights reserved. Used by permission of Crossroad Publishing Co.

Proper 21

Andrew Young, *A Way Out of No Way* (Nashville: Thomas Nelson Publishers, 1994), 2.

Jacob Lawrence, *Harriet and the Promised Land* (New York: Windmill Books, Inc., 1968). Copyright © 1968, 1993 Jacob Lawrence. Reprinted by permission of Simon and Schuster Books for Young Readers.

Joseph Campbell and Bill Moyers, *The Power of Myth*, ed. Betty Sue Flowers (New York: Doubleday, 1988), 5. Used by permission of Doubleday, a division of Bantam Dell Doubleday Publishing Group, Inc.

Lavon Bayler, *Fresh Winds of the Spirit, Book 2: Liturgical Resources for Year A* (Cleveland, Ohio: The Pilgrim Press, 1992), 120. Used by permission.

Proper 22

Tony, age 11, in Robert Coles, *The Spiritual Life of Children* (Boston: Houghton Mifflin Co., 1990), 262. All rights reserved. Used by permission.

John Updike, "Lifeguard," in *Voices from the Heart: Four Centuries of American Piety* (New York: Eerdmans, 1987), 387. Used by permission.

Don Browning, *The Moral Context of Pastoral Care* (Philadelphia: Westminster Press, 1976).

Exodus 20:1–17 and Mark 12:29–31, adapted, *United Church of Christ Book of Worship* (New York: United Church of Christ Office for Church Life and Leadership, 1986), 280, 517. Used by permission.

Moses Maimonides (1135–1204), *Yad Hazakah, Hilkhot Shabbat* 2:3.

"Psalm 19," in *A Book of Psalms, Selected and Adapted from the Hebrew*, trans. Stephen Mitchell (San Francisco: HarperCollins, 1993), 10–11. Used by permission.

Proper 23

Fred Craddock, *Preaching Through the Christian Year, Year B: A Comprehensive Commentary of the Lectionary*, ed. Fred B. Craddock, John H. Hayes, Carl R. Holladay, and Gene M. Tucker (Valley Forge, Pa.: Trinity Press International, 1993), 475.

R. C. D. Jasper and G. J. Cuming, "Invitation to Communion," in *Prayers of the Eucharist: Early and Reformed* (New York: Oxford University Press, 1980), 173.

Susan A. Blain, "A Preaching Dress Sermon," James Memorial Chapel, Union Theological Seminary, New York City, October 16, 1987. Used by permission.

Charles Singer, "Change," in *Gospel Prayers* (Strasbourg, France: Editions du Signe, 1992), 43. Used by permission.

Proper 24

St. Augustine, *St. Augustine on the Psalms*, adapted and translated by Dame Scholastica Hebin and Dame Fekucutas Corrigan (New York: Newman Press, n.d.). Used by permission of Paulist Press.

All in the Family, CBS Television Network, New York, N.Y.

Joseph G. Donders, *Jesus the Stranger: Reflections on the Gospel* (Maryknoll, N.Y.: Orbis Books, 1978). Used by permission of the poet.

Marcia Lee Falk, *Song of Songs: A New Translation and Interpretation* (San Francisco: Harper and Row, 1990), 28. © 1973, 1977, 1982, 1990 by Marcia Lee Falk. Used by permission of HarperCollins Publishers, Inc.

Proper 25

M. Douglas Meeks, "Love and the Hope for a Just Society," in Frederic B. Burnham, Charles McCoy, and M. Douglas Meeks, *Love: The Foundation in the Theology of Jürgen Moltmann and Elizabeth Moltmann-Wendel* (San Francisco: Harper & Row, 1988), 44–45.

"A Sioux Prayer," in *The HarperCollins Book of Prayers*, ed. Robert Van de Weyer (San Francisco: HarperCollins, 1993), 322. Used by permission of HarperCollins Publishers, Inc.

James L. Mays, *Psalms Interpretation: A Bible Commentary for Teaching and Preaching Sermons* (Louisville: Westminster/John Knox Press, 1994), 294–95.

Maya Angelou, *All God's Children Need Traveling Shoes* (New York: Random House, 1986), 83.

D. H. Lawrence, "Pax," in *The Complete Poems of D. H. Lawrence*, ed. Vivian de Sola Pinto and F. Warren Roberts (New York: Viking Press, 1964), 1:153. Copyright © 1964, 1971 by Angelo Ravagli and C. M. Weekley, Executives of the Estate of Frieda Lawrence Ravagli. Used by permission of Viking Penguin, a division of Penguin Books USA, Inc.

David Haas, "You Are Mine," copyright © 1991 by G. I. A. Publications, Inc., Chicago, IL (Admin ICG). All rights reserved. Used by permission.

Proper 26

James L. Mays, *Psalms Interpretation: A Bible Commentary for Teaching and Preaching Sermons* (Louisville: Westminster/John Knox Press, 1994), 347.

Christina Rossetti, "Up-Hill," in *The New Oxford Book of English Verse* (New York: Oxford University Press, 1972), 725.

Anonymous, "Souls Piled Up Like Timber," in *God Struck Me Dead: Voices of Ex-Slaves*, ed. Clifton H. Johnson (Cleveland, Ohio: The Pilgrim Press, 1993), 96–97.

Pierre Talec, *Bread in the Desert*, trans. Edmond Bonin (New York: Newman Press, 1973), 83. Used by permission of Paulist Press.

All Saints' Day

Maya Angelou, excerpt from "Ailey, Baldwin, Floyd, Killens and Mayfield," in *I Shall Not Be Moved* (New York: Random House, 1990). Copyright © 1990 by Maya Angelou. Used by permission of Random House, Inc., and the Helen Brann Agency.

"The Saints Are Standing Row on Row," translated from the Dutch by Gracia Grindal, in *Liturgy: All Saints Among the Churches* 12, no. 2 (Fall 1994), of *Liturgy: The Journal of the Liturgical Conference*. © The Liturgical Conference. All rights reserved. Used by permission.

Theophane Venard, "Be Merry," in *The Wisdom of the Saints: An Anthology*, ed. Jill Haak Adels (New York: Oxford University Press, 1987).

Proper 27

Bob Dylan, excerpt from "Gotta Serve Somebody," Special Rider Music, © 1979. Used by permission.

Paulo Solari, "Choose, Choose, Choose," in *Journal for Current Social Issues*.

Robert Frost, "The Road Not Taken," in *New England Anthology of Robert Frost's Poems* (New York: Washington Square Press, 1971), 223. Used by permission of Henry Holt & Co.

Therese Martin, *The Story of a Soul: The Autobiography of St. Therese of Lisieux*, trans. John Beevers (New York: Doubleday and Co., 1961). Used by permission of Doubleday, a division of the Bantam Doubleday Dell Publishing Group, Inc.

"O Lord Our God," in National Council of Churches of the Philippines, *Fourteenth Biennial Convention Resource Book* (Manila: National Council of Churches of the Philippines, 1989). Used by permission.

Proper 28

Fred B. Craddock, *Preaching Through the Christian Year, Year B: A Comprehensive Commentary of the Lectionary*, ed. Fred B. Craddock, John H. Hayes, Carl R. Holladay, and Gene M. Tucker (Valley Forge, Pa.: Trinity Press International, 1993), 515.

Antonio Machado, "The Wind, One Brilliant Day," in *Times Alone: Selected Poems by Antonio Machado*, trans. Robert Bly (Hanover, N.H.: Wesleyan University Press, 1983). Copyright 1983 by Robert Bly. Used by permission of Robert Bly.

Grant Spradling, *End of the Road*, unpublished manuscript. Used by permission.

Langston Hughes, "Harlem," in *The Panther and the Lash* (New York: Alfred A. Knopf, 1967), 4. Copyright 1932 by Alfred A. Knopf, renewed 1958 by Langston Hughes. Reprinted by permission of the publisher and Harold Ober Associates, Inc.

Bridget Rees, "O God, You Claim Me," in *Bread of Tomorrow: Prayers for the Church Year*, ed. Janet Morley (Maryknoll, N.Y.: Orbis Books, 1992), 64. Used by permission.

Proper 29

Stanley Hauerwas and William H. Willimon, *Resident Aliens* (Nashville: Abingdon Press, 1989), 83–84. Used by permission.

James Weldon Johnson, "The Judgment Day," in *God's Trombones: Seven Negro Sermons in Verse* (New York: Viking Press, 1955), 55–56. Copyright 1927 by Viking Press, Inc., renewed 1955 by Grace Nail Johnson. Used by permission of Viking Penguin, a division of Penguin Books USA, Inc.

Robert W. Castle, Jr., "As You Did It to One of the Least of These My Brethren," in *The Wideness of God's Mercy*, ed. Jeffrey W. Rowthorn (Minneapolis: Seabury Press, 1985), 2:164–65. Used by permission.

Advent 1

Lamar Williamson, Jr., *Interpretation: Mark* (Louisville: John Knox Press, 1983).

Czeslaw Milosz, "A Song on the End of the World," Warsaw, 1944, trans. Anthony Milosz, in *Selected Poems* (New York: Seabury Press, 1973), 57. Used by permission of HarperCollins Publishers, Inc.

Arthur G. Clyde, "Keep Awake, Be Always Ready," in *The New Century Hymnal* (Cleveland, Ohio: The Pilgrim Press, 1995), no. 112. Copyright © 1993 by The Pilgrim Press. Used by permission.

Janet Morley, in *Bread of Tomorrow: Prayers for the Church Year*, ed. Janet Morley (Maryknoll, N.Y.: Orbis Books, 1992), 23. Used by permission of Janet Morley.

Sandra Cisneros, *The House on Mango Street* (New York: Viking Books, 1991), 33.

"The Gelasian Sacramentary," in *The HarperCollins Book of Prayers*, ed. Robert Van de Weyer (San Francisco: HarperCollins, 1993), 165. Used by permission of HarperCollins Publishers, Inc.

Advent 2

Richard D. N. Dickinson, "Advent: Expectancy but with Costs," in *Social Themes of the Christian Year*, ed. Dieter T. Hessel (Philadelphia: The Geneva Press, 1983), 44.

Joseph G. Donders, *The Jesus Community: Reflections on the Gospels for the B-Cycle* (Maryknoll, N.Y.: Orbis Books, 1981), 12–13. Used by permission of the author.

Thomas H. Troeger and Carol Doran, "Wild Man and Wild the Place," in *New Hymns for the Lectionary* (New York: Oxford University Press, 1986), no. 36. Used by permission.

Anonymous, "Che Jesus," in *In Essentials, Unity*, ed. Edward A. Powers (New York: Friendship Press, 1982), 60–61.

Rainer Maria Rilke, *Letters to a Young Poet*, trans. M. D. Herter Norton (New York: W. W. Norton & Co., 1934), 51. Used by permission.

Advent 3

"Ute Prayer," in *Earth Prayers from Around the World* (San Francisco: HarperCollins, 1991), 176.

Lucille Clifton, "Spring Song," in *Good Woman: Poems and a Memoir 1969–1980* (Brockport, N.Y.: BOA Editions, Ltd., 1987). Copyright © 1987 by Lucille Clifton. Used by permission of BOA Editions, 92 Park Avenue, Brockport, N.Y. 14420.

Meister Eckhart, in *Meditations with Meister Eckhart*, introductions and versions by Matthew Fox (Santa Fe, N.M.: Bear and Co., 1983). Used by permission.

John H. Hayes, "Third Sunday in Advent," in *Preaching Through the Christian Year, Year B: A Comprehensive Commentary of the Lectionary*, ed. Fred B. Craddock, John H. Hayes, Carl R. Holladay, and Gene M. Tucker (Valley Forge, Pa.: Trinity Press International, 1993), 15.

Advent 4

Walter Burghart, *Sir, We Would like to See Jesus: Homilies from a Hilltop* (New York: Paulist Press, 1982), 140.

"Selected Praises of Mary from the Agathestos Hymn," in *Mother of God,* ed. Lawrence Cunningham (San Francisco: Harper & Row, 1982), 123. Used by permission of HarperCollins Publishers, Inc.

Kathleen Norris, "Advent," in *Cries of the Spirit: A Celebration of Women's Spirituality* (Boston: Beacon Press, 1991), 63. Copyright © Kathleen Norris. Used by permission of the author.

Janet Morley, "Sing Out My Soul," in *All Desires Known,* expanded edition (Harrisburg, Pa.: Morehouse Publishing, 1992), 76. Used by permission.

Christmas

Janet Morley, "A Eucharistic Prayer for Christmas Eve," in *All Desires Known,* expanded edition (Harrisburg, Pa.: Morehouse Publishing, 1992), 48–49. Used by permission.

"Welcome, Welcome Jesus Christ Our Infant Savior," in *A New Zealand Prayer Book: He Karakia Mihinare o Aotearoa* (Auckland, New Zealand: William Collins Publishers, Ltd., 1989), 527. Used by permission.

Christmas 1

Madeleine L'Engle, *The Glorious Impossible* (New York: Simon and Schuster, 1990), 7.

Daniel H. Evans, "Looking for Incarnation," in *Alive Now!*, November/December 1985, 61. Used by permission.

Helen Flexner, quoted in Maria Harris, *Dance of the Spirit: The Seven Steps of Women's Spirituality* (New York: Bantam Books, 1989). Used by permission of Bantam Doubleday Dell Publishing Group, Inc.

Mani Leib, "From the Crag," in *Voices within the Ark: The Modern Jewish Poets,* ed. Howard Schwartz and Anthony Rudolf (New York: Avon Books, 1980), 298. Translations © 1979 David G. Roskies. Used by permission of David G. Roskies.

Rudolf A. Anaya, *Bless Me, Ultima* (Berkeley: TQS Publications, 1991), 38.

"Nunc Dimittis (Song of Simeon)," in *The New Century Hymnal* (Cleveland, Ohio: The Pilgrim Press, 1995), no. 808. Reprinted from the *United Church of Christ Book of Worship* (New York: United Church of Christ Office of Church Life and Leadership, 1986). Copyright © 1986. Used by permission.

Christmas 2

Patricia Wilson-Kastner, *Faith, Feminism, and the Christ* (Philadelphia: Fortress Press, 1983), 90. Used by permission of Augsburg Fortress Press.

Antonio Machado, "Last Night," in *Times Alone: Selected Poems of Antonio Machado,* trans. Robert Bly (Hanover, N.H.: Wesleyan University Press, 1983). © 1983 by Robert Bly. Used by permission of Robert Bly.

Clement of Alexandria, "Exhortation," in Jaroslav Pelikan, *Jesus Through the Centuries: His Place in the History of Culture* (New York: HarperCollins Publishers, 1987), 39.

Huub Oosterhuis, "Your Heart Goes Out," in *Your Word Is Near,* trans. N. D. Smith (New York: Paulist Press, 1968), 51. Used by permission.

Epiphany

Peter Chrysogolus, "In Choosing to Be Born for Us," in *A Christmas Sourcebook,* ed. Mary Ann Simcoe (Chicago: Liturgy Training Publications, 1984), 108.

"Collect for the Season of Epiphany," in *A New Zealand Prayer Book: He Karakia Mihinare o Aotearoa* (Auckland, New Zealand: William Collins Publishers, Ltd., 1989), 560. Used by permission.

Jan Berry, "God of Gold," in *Bread of Tomorrow: Prayers for the Church Year,* ed. Janet Morley (Maryknoll, N.Y.: Orbis Books, 1992), 51. Used by permission.

Epiphany 1

Henri Nouwen, *Life of the Beloved: Spiritual Living in a Secular World* (New York: Crossroad Publishing, 1993), 106.

Langston Hughes, "The Negro Speaks of Rivers," in *Selected Poems* (New York: Alfred A. Knopf, Inc. 1926). © 1926 by Alfred A. Knopf, Inc., and renewed 1954 by Langston Hughes. Reprinted by permission of the publisher and Harold Ober Associates, Inc.

Joseph G. Donders, "Stepping in the Mud," in *Jesus the Stranger* (Maryknoll, N.Y.: Orbis Books, 1978), 18–21. Used by permission of the poet.

Thomas H. Troeger, "What Ruler Wades Through Murky Streams" (New York: Oxford University Press). Words Copyright © 1984; rev. 1993, Oxford University Press, Inc. Music Copyright © 1993 The Pilgrim Press. Used by permission.

Epiphany 2

Sören Kierkegaard, as quoted by Joachim Berendt in *The Third Ear* (Shaftsbury, England: Element Books, 1988). Used by permission.

The Eerdman's Bible Dictionary, ed. Allen Myers (Grand Rapids, Mich.: Eerdmans's Publishing Co., 1987), 909.

Isak Dinesen, *Out of Africa* (New York: Random House, 1965).

R.E.M., "These Days," from *Life's Rich Pageant* (International Records Syndicate, 1986). Used by permission.

Anonymous Indonesian author, "In the Depth of Silence," in *Bread of Tomorrow: Prayers for the Church Year*, ed. Janet Morley (Maryknoll, N.Y.: Orbis Books, 1992), 124.

Epiphany 3

Jeff Melvoin, "Fish Story," episode 18, from *Northern Exposure* (Studio City, CA: Pipeline Productions, 1993), 45, 46–47.

Thomas Reese, "The Prayer of Jonah," in *Peace Prayers from Around the World* (San Francisco: HarperCollins Publishers, 1992), 6–7.

Elie Wiesel, "Jonah," in *Five Biblical Portraits* (South Bend, Ind.: University of Notre Dame Press, 1981), 150–51.

Carl Sandburg, "Losers," in *Complete Poems* (New York: Harcourt, Brace & World, 1950), 189. Used by permission.

Epiphany 4

Dan Wakefield, "Miracles Then and Now," in *Image: A Journal of the Arts and Religion*, no. 9 (Spring 1995), 109.

Etty Hillesum, *An Interrupted Life: The Diaries of Etty Hillesum, 1941–1943* (New York: Washington Square Press, 1981).

Rita Nakashima Brock, *Journeys by Heart: A Christology of Erotic Power* (New York: Crossroad Publishing, 1988), 80–81.

Gerd Theissen, *The Miracle Stories of the Early Christian Tradition* (Philadelphia: Fortress Press, 1983), 302.

"Prayer of Thanksgiving," in *United Church of Christ Book of Worship* (New York: United Church of Christ Office for Church Life and Leadership, 1986), 319–20. Used by permission.

Epiphany 5

John D. W. Watts, *Isaiah 34–66* (Waco, Tex.: Word Books Publishers, 1987), 95–96.

Maya Angelou, excerpt from "The Caged Bird," in *Shaker, Why Don't You Sing?* (New York: Random House, 1983). Copyright © 1983 by Maya Angelou. Used by permission of Random House, Inc., and the Helen Brann Agency.

Joy Harjo, "Eagle Poem," in *Cries of the Spirit: A Celebration of Women's Spirituality*, ed. Marilyn Sewell (Boston: Beacon Press, 1991). Copyright © 1990 by Joy Harjo. Used by permission of Wesleyan University Press.

Hindu prayer, "You Are, O God," in *Prayers, Praises and Thanksgivings* (New York: Dial Books, 1992).

Tony Proscio, "Religion and the Corruption of Faith," *The Miami Herald*, September 25, 1994.

Melanie Beattie, *The Language of Letting Go* (New York: HarperCollins Publishing, 1990), 6. Used by permission.

Proper 1 (Epiphany 6)

Artur Weiser, "Psalm 30," in *The Psalms, A Commentary*, trans. Herbert Hartwell (Philadelphia: Westminster Press, 1962), 272.

Thomas Merton, *New Seeds of Contemplation* (New York: New Directions Publishers, 1961), 297.

"Fount of All Life, Dancing in Bliss," from United Theological College, Bangalore, India, in *Bread of Tomorrow: Prayers for the Church Year*, ed. Janet Morley (Maryknoll, N.Y.: Orbis Books, 1992), 134. Used by permission.

Zephania Kameeta, "Psalm 26," in *Why, O Lord?* (Geneva: World Council of Churches, 1986). Used by permission.

Proper 2 (Epiphany 7)

Fred B. Craddock, *Preaching Through the Christian Year, Year B: A Comprehensive Commentary of the Lectionary*, ed. Fred B. Craddock, John H. Hayes, Carl R. Holladay, and Gene M. Tucker (Valley Forge, Pa.: Trinity Press International, 1993), 105–6.

Michele Najilis, "We Are Children of the Sun Are We," in *Lovers and Comrades*, ed. Amanda Hopkinson (New York: Women's Press, 1989). Used by permission of Interlink Publishing Group, Inc.

Martin Buber, *Between Man and Man* (Boston: Beacon Press, 1955), 70.

Prayer for Nicaragua, "May It Come Soon," in *Windows into Worship*, ed. Ron Ingamells (Champaign, Ill.: YMCA Publishers, 1989). Used by permission of the National Council of YMCAs of England.

D. J. Butler, Key West Metropolitan Community Church Worship Service, Key West, Florida. Used by permission.

Proper 3 (Epiphany 8)

Brian Wren, "The Church," in *The New Century Hymnal* (Cleveland, Ohio: The Pilgrim Press, 1995), no. 309. Lyrics © 1975 by Hope Publishing Co., Carol Stream, Illinois. Used by permission.

Marcus J. Borg, *Meeting Jesus Again for the First Time* (New York: HarperCollins Publishers, 1995), 55.

Rilla Askew, *Strange Business* (New York: Penguin Books, 1993), 136–38. © 1992 by Rilla Askew. Used by permission of Viking Penguin, a division of Penguin Books USA, Inc.

Ann Asper Wilson, "People of God," in *United Church of Christ Book of Worship* (New York: United Church of Christ Office for Church Life and Leadership, 1986). Used by permission.

Transfiguration Sunday

Kathryn Spink, *A Universal Heart* (San Francisco: Harper & Row, 1988).

Madeleine L'Engle, *The Irrational Season* (New York: Seabury Press, 1977), 194. Copyright © 1977 by Crosswicks, Ltd. Used by permission of Lescher & Lescher.

Jonathan Edwards, *The Works of President Edwards*, vol. 1 (New York: S. Converse, 1829), 133–34.

Alice Walker, "The Welcome Table," in *In Love and Trouble: Stories of Black Women* (New York: Harcourt, Brace and Co., 1970), 43. Used by permission.

Ash Wednesday

Marie Howe, "What the Living Do," in *Atlantic Monthly*, April 1994, 68. Used by permission.

J. Raya and J. de Vinck, "Verses During the Last Kiss: Funeral of the Dead," in *Byzantine Daily Worship* (Allendale, N.J.: Alleluia Press, 1988). Used by permission.

Walker Percy, *Lost in the Cosmos: The Last Self-Help Book* (New York: Farrar, Straus & Giroux, 1983).

Ansarit of Herat, *The Invocations of Sheik Ansarit of Herat*, trans. Sardar Sir Jogendra Singh (London: n.p., 1939).

Lent 1

John H. Hayes, *Preaching Through the Christian Year, Year B: A Comprehensive Commentary of the Lectionary*, ed. Fred B. Craddock, John H. Hayes, Carl R. Holladay, and Gene M. Tucker (Valley Forge, Pa.: Trinity Press International, 1993), 137.

Havatselet Levi, "Signs," in *My Shalom, My Peace*, ed. Jacob Zim (New York: McGraw Hill Book Co., 1975), 93. English translation © 1975 by Sabra Books, Tel Aviv. Used by permission.

Jaroslav Vajda, "God of the Sparrow God of the Whale," in *The New Century Hymnal* (Cleveland, Ohio: Pilgrim Press, 1995), no. 32. Words Copyright © 1983 by Jaroslav J. Vajda. Used by permission.

Carmen Bernos De Gasztold, "Noah's Prayer," in *Prayers from the Ark*, trans. Rumer Godden (New York: Viking Press, 1962), 13. Translation copyright © 1962, renewed 1990 by Rumer Godden. Original copyright 1947, © 1955 by Editions du Cloitre. Used by permission of Viking Penguin, a division of Penguin Books USA, Inc.

Lent 2

Fred B. Craddock, *Preaching Through the Christian Year, Year B: A Comprehensive Commentary of the Lectionary*, ed. Fred B. Craddock, John H. Hayes, Carl R. Holladay, and Gene M. Tucker (Valley Forge, Pa.: Trinity Press International, 1993), 143.

The Color Purple, book by Alice Walker, screenplay by Menno Meyjes. Program content, artwork, and photography © 1985 by Warner Brothers.

Antoine de Saint-Exupery, *The Little Prince*, trans. Katharine Woods (New York: Harcourt Brace Jovanovich, 1943), 80–84. Copyright renewed 1971 by Harcourt Brace Jovanovich, Inc. Used by permission.

"Blessing of the Wedding Rings," in *United Church of Christ Book of Worship* (New York: United Church of Christ Office for Church Life and Leadership, 1986), 335. Used by permission.

"A Covenant Prayer in the Wesleyan Tradition," in *The United Methodist Hymnal, Book of United Methodist Worship* (Nashville: The United Methodist Publishing House, 1989), 607.

Lent 3

Raymond E. Brown, *The Gospel According to John: 1–12* (Garden City, N.J.: Doubleday & Co., 1966), 121.

Beverly Harrison, "The Power of Anger in the Work of Love," in *Making the Connections: Essays in Feminist Social Ethics* (Boston: Beacon Press, 1985).

Herman Melville, *Moby Dick* (New York: Bantam Books, 1867), 53.

Marge Piercy, "A Just Anger," in *Circles on the Water* (New York: Alfred A. Knopf, 1982). Copyright © 1982 by Marge Piercy. Used by permission.

Yong Ting Jin, "We Believe in Jesus Christ," in *Bread of Tomorrow: Prayers for the Church Year*, ed. Janet Morley (Maryknoll, N.Y.: Orbis Books, 1992), 137. Used by permission.

Lent 4

Benjamin Chavis, Jr., "Psalm 132," in *Psalms from Prison* (Cleveland, Ohio: The Pilgrim Press, 1994), 149. Used by permission.

Choan-Seng Song, *Theology from the Womb of Asia* (Maryknoll, N.Y.: Orbis Books, 1979), 199. Used by permission.

Alice Walker, *Possessing the Secret of Joy* (New York: Simon and Schuster, 1992), 275–76.

Madeleine L'Engle, "My Bath," in *Everyday Prayers* (Ridgefield, Conn.: Morehouse-Barlow). Copyright © 1974 by Crosswicks, Ltd. Used by permission of Lescher and Lescher.

Lent 5

Fred B. Craddock, *Preaching Through the Christian Year, Year B: A Comprehensive Commentary of the Lectionary*, ed. Fred B. Craddock, John H. Hayes, Carl R. Holladay, and Gene M. Tucker (Valley Forge, Pa.: Trinity Press International, 1993), 161, 162.

Arthur Miller, *The Creation of the World*, in *Collected Plays*, vol. 2 (New York: Viking Press, 1981), 441.

Palm/Passion Sunday

Shusaku Endo, *A Life of Jesus*, trans. Richard A. Schuchert (New York: Paulist Press, 1978), 106–8. Used by permission.

John Leax, "Lent," in *Stories for the Christian Year: The Chrysostom Society*, ed. Eugene H. Peterson (New York: Macmillan, 1992), 95.

Lucy Bregman, *Homily Service* (Washington, D.C.: Liturgical Conference, 1989).

Leonardo Boff, *Way of the Cross, Way of Justice* (Maryknoll, N.Y.: Orbis Books, 1980). Used by permission.

"Collect for Palm Sunday," in *A New Zealand Prayer Book: He Karakia Mihinare o Aotearoa* (Auckland, New Zealand: William Collins Publishers, Ltd., 1989), 581. Used by permission.

Holy Thursday

George Ella Lyon, "The Foot Washing," in *Appalachian Journal* 9, no. 4 (Summer 1982). © 1982 Appalachian State University/*Appalachian Journal* Summer 1982 (vol. 9:4). Used by permission.

Workers in Community Soup Kitchens, Lima, Peru, "God, Food of the Poor," in *Bread of Tomorrow: Prayers for the Church Year*, ed. Janet Morley (Maryknoll, N.Y.: Orbis Books, 1992), 85. Used by permission of SPCK and Latinamerica Press.

Good Friday

Miriam Kessler, "Eli, Eli," in *Cries of the Spirit: A Celebration of Women's Spirituality*, ed. Marilyn Sewell (Boston: Beacon Press, 1991), 256. Copyright © by Miriam Kessler.

Patricia Wilson-Kastner, *Faith, Feminism and the Christ* (Philadelphia: Fortress Press, 1983), 100.

St. Ignatius of Loyola, *The Spiritual Exercises of St. Ignatius*, trans. Louis Puhl (Chicago: Loyola University Press, 1951), 1.

E. E. Cummings, from *Xiape* (New York: Harcourt Brace Jovanovich, 1950). Copyright © 1950 by the Trustees of the E. E. Cummings Trust. Used by permission of Liveright Publishing Corp.

Shusaku Endo, *A Life of Jesus*, trans. Richard A. Schuchert (New York: Paulist Press, 1978), 147. Used by permission.

Easter

Janet Morley, "When We Are All Despairing," in *Bread of Tomorrow: Prayers for the Church Year* (Maryknoll, N.Y.: Orbis Books, 1992), 117. Used by permission.

Mary Gordon, "The Gospel According to Mark," in *Incarnation: Contemporary Writers on the New Testament* (New York: Viking Press, 1990), 24.

Annie Dillard, *Teaching a Stone to Talk: Expeditions and Encounters* (New York: Harper and Row, 1982), 141.

Denise Levertov, "Cancion," in *The Freeing of the Dust* (New York: New Directions Publishing Co., 1975), 21. © 1975 by Denise Levertov. Used by permission of New Directions Publishing Corp.

Janet Morley, "God of Terror and Joy," in *All Desires Known: Prayers Uniting Faith and Feminism* (Wilton, Conn.: Morehouse-Barlow, 1988), 16. Used by permission.

Easter 2

Fred B. Craddock, *Preaching Through the Christian Year, Year B: A Comprehensive Commentary of the Lectionary*, ed. Fred B. Craddock, John H. Hayes, Carl R. Holladay, and Gene M. Tucker (Valley Forge, Pa.: Trinity Press International, 1993), 238.

"A Preacher from a God-fearing Plantation," in *God Struck Me Dead: Voices of Ex-Slaves*, ed. Clifton H. Johnson (Cleveland, Ohio: The Pilgrim Press, 1993), 90.

United Church of Canada, "A New Creed," in *All Year Round* (London: British Council of Churches, 1988). Used by permission.

Iona Community, "We Have Heard About You," in *A Wee Worship Book* (Glasgow: Wild Goose Publications, 1989). Used by permission.

Easter 3

Paul Hammer, "The Background Word," in *The Inviting Word: A Worship-centered, Lectionary-based Curriculum for the Whole Congregation* Leader's Guides (Cleveland, Ohio: United Church Press, 1996). Used by permission.

John Shelby Spong, *Rescuing the Bible from Fundamentalism* (San Francisco: HarperCollins Publishers, 1992), 226–30.

"Haleluya! Pelo tsa rona (Halleluya! We Sing Your Praises)," in *The New Century Hymnal* (Cleveland, Ohio: The Pilgrim Press, 1995). Copyright © Walton Music Corporation. Used by permission.

"Creed from Nicaraguan Mass," in *Bread of Tomorrow: Prayers for the Church Year*, ed. Janet Morley (Maryknoll, N.Y.: Orbis Books, 1992), 106–7.

Easter 4

Rosemary Radford Ruether, *To Change the World: Christology and Cultural Criticism* (New York: Crossroad Publishing, 1981), 27–28. Used by permission.

Archbishop Oscar Romero, in James R. Brockman, *The Word Remains: A Life of Oscar Romero* (Maryknoll, N.Y.: Orbis Books, 1982), 223. Used by permission.

Anna May Say Pa, "For the People," in *Prayers, Poems, Songs and Stories: Churches in Solidarity with Women Ecumenical Decade 1988–1998* (Geneva: WCC Publications, 1988), 18. Used by permission.

Maurice Sendak, "Jack and Guy Went Out in the Rye," in *We Are All in the Dumps with Jack and Guy* (New York: HarperCollins Publishers, 1993), unpaginated. © 1993 by Maurice Sendak. Used by permission of HarperCollins Publishers, Inc.

"Invocation," in *United Church of Christ Book of Worship* (New York: United Church of Christ Office for Church Life and Leadership, 1986), 491. Used by permission.

Easter 5

Pierre Talec, *Bread in the Desert*, trans. Edmond Bonin (New York: Newman Press, 1973), 78. Used by permission of Paulist Press.

D. Moody Smith, "John," in *Harper's Bible Commentary*, ed. James L. Mays (San Francisco: Harper & Row, 1988), 1068–69.

Catherine of Siena, "Prayer 17," in *The Prayers of Catherine of Siena*, ed. Suzanne Noffke (New York: Paulist Press, 1983), 149, 151, lines 86–88, 170–77. Used by permission.

Miriam Therese Winter, "Roots," in *God-with-Us: Resources for Prayer and Praise* (Nashville: Abingdon Press, 1979), 85. © Medical Mission Sisters, Philadelphia, Pa. Used by permission.

Easter 6

Quandra Prettyman, "When Mahalia Sings," in *I Am the Darker Brother: An Anthology of Modern Poems by Negro Americans* (New York: Macmillan, 1968), 56–57. Used by permission.

August Wilson, *Ma Rainey's Black Bottom* (New York: New American Library, 1985), 83. Copyright © 1985 by August Wilson. Used by permission of Dutton Signet, a division of Penguin Books USA, Inc.

Martin Buber, *Tales of the Hasidim: The Masters*, trans. Olga Perlzweig (New York: Random House, 1947).

"Come on Children, Let's Sing" as recorded by Mahalia Jackson, Copyright © 1991 by Sony Music Entertainment Corporation. Used by permission.

Easter 7

Jennifer Glenn, "An Introduction to the Liturgy of the Hours," in *Psalms for Morning and Evening Prayer* (Chicago: Archdiocese of Chicago, Liturgy Training Publications, 1995), xxiii–xxvi.

Miriam Therese Winter, *WomanWord: A Feminist Lectionary and Psalter: Women of the New Testament* (New York: Crossroad, 1990), 260. Copyright © 1990 by Medical Mission Sisters. All rights reserved. Used by permission of Crossroad Publishing.

"Prayer for Unity in Christ," Cornerstone Community Church, Belfast, Northern Ireland. Used by permission.

Annie Dillard, *Teaching a Stone to Talk: Expeditions and Encounters* (New York: Harper & Row, 1982), 76.

Thomas Carver, *George Tooker* (New York: Marisa del Re Gallery, 1988), 3.

Pentecost Sunday

Bianco da Siena, "Come Down, O Love Divine," trans. Richard Frederick Littledale, in *The Presbyterian Hymnal* (Louisville: Westminster/John Knox Press, 1990), no. 313. Used by permission.

"A Litany for Pentecost," from *Models for Ministers I*, in *The Wideness of God's Mercy*, ed. Jeffrey W. Rowthorn (Minneapolis: Seabury Press, 1985), 1:126–127.

Osvaldo Catena, "Soplo de Dios Viviente," in *The New Century Hymnal* (Cleveland, Ohio: The Pilgrim Press, 1995), no. 56. Spanish Copyright © Osvaldo Catena. Translation Copyright © 1993 by The Pilgrim Press. Used by permission.

Trinity Sunday (Pentecost 1)

Edmund A. Steimle, "God Far—God Near," in *God the Stranger* (Philadelphia: Fortress Press, 1979), 46. Used by permission of Augsburg Fortress Press.

"O Light! Divine and One Holy Trinity," *Matin Hymn, Armenian Sunrise Office*, as cited in *In Spirit and in Truth* (Geneva: WCC Publications, 1991), 2. Used by permission of WCC Publications.

Catherine of Siena, "Sea, Light, Fire," from *The Dialogue*, in *The HarperCollins Book of Prayers*, ed. Robert Van de Weyer (San Francisco: Harper San Francisco, 1993), 89–90. Used by permission of Paulist Press.

Michael Shaw and Paul Indwood, "Litany of the Spirit," (London: St. Thomas More Centre, 1978) as quoted in *In Spirit and in Truth* (Geneva: WCC Publications, 1991), 7. Used by permission.

Brian Wren, "How Wonderful the Three-in-One," Hope Publishing Co., Carol Stream IL, 1989. Used by permission.

Proper 4

Paul Tillich, "Address on the Occasion of the Opening of the New Galleries and Sculpture Garden of the Museum of Modern Art," in *On Art and Architecture*, ed. John Dillenberger and Jane Dillenberger (New York: Crossroad, 1987), 247.

Letty M. Russell, *The Future of Partnership* (Philadelphia: The Westminster Press, 1979), 106.

George F. MacLeod, excerpt from "The Cost of a Changing Day," in *The Whole Earth Shall Cry Glory* (Glasgow: Wild Goose Publications, 1985), 21. Used by permission.

Stephen Orchard, "Come Holy Spirit," in *All the Glorious Names: United Reformed Church Prayer Handbook* (London, 1989), quoted in *Bread of Tomorrow: Prayers for the Church Year*, ed. Janet Morley (Maryknoll, N.Y.: Orbis Books, 1992), 127. Used by permission of the United Reformed Church.

Proper 5

Carl R. Holladay, *Preaching Through the Christian Year, Year B: A Comprehensive Commentary of the Lectionary*, ed. Fred B. Craddock, John H. Hayes, Carl R. Holladay, and Gene M. Tucker (Valley Forge, Pa.: Trinity Press International, 1993), 303.

Roger L. Shinn, "Statement of Faith, the Revision of 1981: A Doxology," in *Confessing Our Faith: An Interpretation of the Statement of Faith of the United Church of Christ* (New York: The Pilgrim Press, 1990), xi. Used by permission.Robert Coles, *The Spiritual Life of Children* (Boston: Houghton Mifflin Co., 1990), 148.

Arthur Rimbaud, excerpt from "Eternity," trans. Francis Golffing, in *Prentice Hall Literature: World Masterpieces* (New York: Prentice Hall, 1991), 910. Originally in *An Anthology of French Poetry from Nerval Valéry in English Translation with French Originals*. Used by permission of Angel Flores.

Proper 6

Carl R. Holladay, in *Preaching Through the Christian Year, Year B: A Comprehensive Commentary of the Lectionary*, ed. Fred B. Craddock, John H. Hayes, Carl R. Holladay, and Gene M. Tucker (Valley Forge, Pa.: Trinity Press International, 1993), 310.

Annie Dillard, *Teaching a Stone to Talk: Expeditions and Encounters* (New York: Harper & Row, 1982), 48–49.

Ben Shahn, "Goya Gets a Guggenheim—Conversations with Ben Shahn," in *As We Are: Seventeen Conversations Between the Americans and the Man from the London Sunday Times*, ed. Henry Brandon Nightmare (New York: Doubleday, 1961), 80.

Dag Hammarskjöld, *Markings*, trans. Leif Sjoberg and W. H. Auden (New York: Alfred A. Knopf, 1966). Translation © 1964 by Alfred A. Knopf, Inc., and Faber & Faber Ltd. Used by permission.

Lai Leng Woon, "I Believe," as cited in Choan-Sent Song, *Third-Eye Theology: Theology in Formation in Asian Settings* (Maryknoll, N.Y.: Orbis Books, 1979), 243. Used by permission.

"Thuma Mina (Send Me Now)," in *The New Century Hymnal* (Cleveland, Ohio: The Pilgrim Press, 1995), no. 360. Copyright © 1984 by Walton Music Corporation. Used by permission.

Proper 7

Mark Link, "Man of Destiny," in *These Stones Will Shout: A New Voice for the Old Testament* (Allen, Tex.: Tabor Publishing, 1983). Copyright © 1983 Mark Link, S.J. Used by permission.

Mary Conway Kohler, *Young People Learning to Care* (New York: Seabury Press), 9.

Carter Heyward, *Staying Power: Reflections on Gender, Justice, and Compassion* (Cleveland, Ohio: The Pilgrim Press, 1995), 67. Used by permission.

Emily Brontë, "No Coward Soul Is Mine," in *The Norton Anthology of Literature by Women*, ed. Sandra M. Gilbert and Susan Gubar (New York: W. W. Norton, 1985), 750.

Proper 8

Philip Zaleski, "The Test of Giving," in *Parabola: The Magazine of Myth and Tradition*, Spring 1991, 20–21.

Iris Murdoch, *The Bell* (London: Triad/Granada, 1981), 235.

John Koenig, *New Testament Hospitality: Partnership with Strangers as Promise and Mission* (Philadelphia: Fortress Press, 1985), 77–78. Used by permission of Augsburg Fortress Press.

David Applebaum, *Everyday Spirits* (Albany, N.Y.: SUNY, 1993), 141.

Chrystos, "Ceremony for Completing a Poetry Reading," in *This Bridge Called My Back: Writings by Radical Women of Color*, ed. Cherrie Moraga and Gloria Anzaldua (New York: Kitchen Table/Women of Color Press, 1983), 191–92. Used by permission.

Proper 9

Fred B. Craddock, in *Preaching Through the Christian Year, Year B: A Comprehensive Commentary of the Lectionary*, ed. Fred B. Craddock, John H. Hayes, Carl R. Holladay, and Gene M. Tucker (Valley Forge, Pa.: Trinity Press International, 1993).

W. H. Auden, "He Is the Way," in *W. H. Auden: Collected Poems*, ed. Edward Mendelson (New York: Random House, 1976). Copyright © 1945 by W. H. Auden. Used by permission of Random House, Inc., and Faber & Faber, Ltd.

"Thuma Mina (Send Me Now)," in *The New Century Hymnal* (Cleveland, Ohio: The Pilgrim Press, 1995), no. 360. Copyright © 1984 by Walton Music Corporation. Used by permission.

Martin B. Copenhaver, *To Begin at the Beginning: An Introduction to the Christian Faith* (Cleveland, Ohio: United Church Press, 1994), 268.

"Go Forth into the World," adapted from *Services of the Church #1*, © 1966 and 1969 United Church Press. Used by permission.

Proper 10

Footloose, 1984 in novel form. Published by Wallaby Books under exclusive license from Paramount Pictures Corporation. © 1984 Paramount Pictures Corporation.

Mechthild of Magdeburg, "I Cannot Dance," in *Women in Praise of the Sacred*, ed. Jane Hirshfield (New York: HarperCollins, 1994), 86.

"Fount of All Life, Dancing in Bliss," from United Theological College, Bangalore, India, in *Bread of Tomorrow: Prayers for the Church Year*, ed. Janet Morley (Maryknoll, N.Y.: Orbis Books, 1992), 134. Used by permission.

Proper 11

"Ojibway Prayer," in *Earth Prayers from Around the World* (San Francisco: HarperSan Francisco, 1991), 95.

Mark Milligan, "Resting in Peace," Wheaton, Illinois. Used by permission of the poet.

Virginia Ramey Mollenkott, *Godding* (New York: Crossroad Publishing, 1987), 38–39.

Jean Vanier, *Community and Growth* (New York: Paulist Press, 1979).

Proper 12

Joseph Donders, excerpt from "One Small Boy," in *The Jesus Community: Reflections on the Gospel for the B-Cycle* (Maryknoll, N.Y.: Orbis Books, 1981), 205. Used by permission of the poet.

Dietrich Bonhoeffer, *Life Together*, trans. John W. Doberstein (San Francisco: Harper & Row, n.d.). Used by permission of HarperCollins Publishers, Inc.

Emily Dickinson, "I Had Been Hungry, All the Years," in *The Poems of Emily Dickinson*, ed. Thomas H. Johnson (Cambridge, Mass.: Harvard University Press, 1951).

Adrienne Rich, excerpt from "Hunger," in *The Dream of a Common Language* (New York: W. W. Norton, 1978), 13. Copyright © 1978 by W. W. Norton & Company, Inc. Used by permission of the author and W. W. Norton & Company, Inc.

Proper 13

Andrew T. Lincoln, *Ephesians* (Waco, Tex.: Word Books, 1990), 267.

Meister Eckhart, in *Meditations with Meister Eckhart*, introductions and versions by Matthew Fox (Santa Fe, N.M.: Bear and Co., 1983). Used by permission.

Teilhard de Chardin, *The Divine Milieu* (New York: Harper Colophon Books, 1960), 64. © 1957 by Editions du Seuill, Paris. English translation © 1960 by Wm. Collins Sons & Co., London, and Harper & Row Publishers, Inc., N.Y. Renewed 1988 by Harper & Row. Used by permission of HarperCollins Publishers, Inc.

"Affirmation of Ministry," in *United Church of Christ Book of Worship* (New York: United Church of Christ Office for Church Life and Leadership, 1986), 433–34. Used by permission.

Proper 14

Simon DeVries, *I Kings* (Waco, Tex.: Word Books, 1985), 236–37.

Etty Hillesum, *An Interrupted Life: The Diaries of Etty Hillesum, 1941–1943* (New York: Washington Square Press, 1981), 238.

Gunilla Norris, "Entering Rest," in *Being Home: A Book of Meditations* (New York: Bell Tower, 1991). Used by permission of Bell Tower Books, a division of Crown Publishers.

Joan M. Burns, "I am here, Lord," in *Prayers, Praises, and Thanksgivings*, comp. Sandol Stoddard (New York: Dial Books, 1992), 45. Used by permission of A. A. Mowbray & Co., Ltd.

Proper 15

Alice Munro, *The Progress of Love* (New York: Alfred A. Knopf, 1986), 4.

Makeda, Queen of Sheba, in *Women in Praise of the Sacred: Forty-three Centuries of Spiritual Poetry by Women*, ed. Jane Hirshfield (New York: HarperCollins, 1994), 13. Used by permission.

Proper 16

Fyodor Dostoyevsky, *The Brothers Karamazov* (New York: New American Library/Penguin Classics, 1982).

John H. Hayes, in *Preaching Through the Christian Year, Year B: A Comprehensive Commentary of the Lectionary*, ed. Fred B. Craddock, John H. Hayes, Carl R. Holladay, and Gene M. Tucker (Valley Forge, Pa.: Trinity Press International, 1993), 383.

"Psalm 84," in *A Book of Psalms: Selected and Adapted from the Hebrew*, trans. Stephen Mitchell (San Francisco: HarperCollins, 1993), 37. Used by permission of HarperCollins Publishers, Inc.

"Blessing of a Home," in *A New Zealand Prayer Book: He Karakia Mihinare o Aotearoa* (Auckland, New Zealand: William Collins, Ltd., 1989), 764, 773. Used by permission.

Proper 17

Helder Camara, *The Desert Is Fertile* (Maryknoll, N.Y.: Orbis Books, 1974). Used by permission.

Paulo Freire, *Pedagogy of the Oppressed*, trans. Myra Bergman Ramos (New York: Continuum Publishing Co., 1993), 69.

Pedro Casaldaliga, "Alleluia," in *Bread of Tomorrow: Prayers for the Church Year*, ed. Janet Morley (Maryknoll, N.Y.: Orbis Books, 1992), 112–13. Used by permission.

Hall Johnson, "Lord I Keep So Busy Praising My Jesus," in *A Lent Sourcebook: The Forty Days, Book Two*, ed. J. Robert Baker, Evelyn Kaehler, and Peter Mazar (Chicago: Liturgy Training Publications, 1990), 3. Used by permission.

Illustration Sources

Foreword

Paul Koli, *The Burning Bush*, in *The Bible Through Asian Eyes*, ed. Masao Takenaka and Ron O'Grady (Auckland, New Zealand: Pace Publishing in association with the Asian Christian Art Association, 1991), 41. Used by permission.

That We May See: An Introduction

Ben Shahn, *The Red Stairway*, St. Louis Art Museum, St. Louis, Mo. © 1996 Estate of Ben Shahn/Licensed by VAGA, New York, N.Y. Used by permission of VAGA.

Max Beckmann, *Landscape, Cannes*, 1934, gift of Louise S. Ackerman, San Francisco Museum of Modern Art, San Francisco, Calif. Used by permission.

Lars Topelman, *Dog and Man Jumping*, Graphistock, New York, N.Y. Used by permission.

Women in Namibia Dancing, Afrapix/Impact Visuals, New York, N.Y. Used by permission.

František Kupka, *Mme. Kupka among Verticals*, 1910–11, oil on canvas, Hillman Periodicals Fund, The Museum of Modern Art, New York, N.Y. Photograph © 1996 The Museum of Modern Art. Used by permission.

Jacob Lawrence, *Harriet and the Promised Land* (New York: Windmill Books, 1968). Copyright © 1968, 1993 Jacob Lawrence. Reprinted by permission of Simon and Schuster Books for Young Readers.

Henry O. Tanner, *The Annunciation*, The W.P. Wilstach Collection, Philadelphia Museum of Art, Philadelphia, Pa. Used by permission.

Playing and Praying: Tips for Engaging Children with Art

Albert Pinkham Ryder, *Jonah*, gift of John Gellatly, National Museum of American Art, Smithsonian Institution, Washington, D.C. (National Museum of American Art, Washington, D.C./Art Resource, N.Y.). Used by permission.

Eliot Porter, *Christ's Entry into Jerusalem, Riding an Ass*, Church of Ixtepec, Oaxaca, dye transfer print, Eliot Porter Collection, Amon Carter Museum, Fort Worth, Tex. © Amon Carter Museum. Used by permission.

Edvard Munch, *The Scream*, Nasjonalgalleriet, Oslo, Norway. Used by permission.

Linda Post, *Solstice*, R. Michelson Galleries, Northampton, Mass. Used by permission of R. Michelson Galleries.

Ben Shahn, *Beatitude*, 1952, private collection. Used by permission of VAGA.

Käthe Kollwitz, *Germany's Children Are Hungry! (Deutschlands Kinder Hungern!)*, 1924 lithograph, Rosenwald Collection, National Gallery of Art, Washington, D.C. Used by permission.

Estelle Ishigo, *Boys with Kite*, Special Collections, University Research Library, UCLA, Los Angeles, Calif. Used by permission.

Mev Puleo, *Presentation, Brazil*, St. Louis, Missouri. Used by permission of the photographer.

Film still from *Footloose*, © 1984 Paramount Pictures. Photo provided by Photofest, New York, N.Y. Used by permission.

Salvador Dali, *Girl Standing at the Window*, Museo d'Arts Contemporanea, Madrid, Spain (Bridgeman/Art Resource, N.Y.). Used by permission.

Mev Puleo, *Girls Praying*, St. Louis, Missouri. Used by permission of the photographer.

Seasonal Divider for Pentecost (Cycle A)

Wassily Kandinsky, *Allerheiligen (All Saints')*, Städtische Galerie im Lenbachhaus, Munich, Germany. Used by permission.

Proper 17

Paul Koli, *The Burning Bush*, as reproduced in *The Bible Through Asian Eyes*, ed. Masao Takenaka and Ron O'Grady (Auckland, New Zealand: Pace Publishing in association with the Asian Christian Art Association, 1991), 41. Used by permission.

Moses on Mount Sinai, from the *Psalter of Ingeburg of Denmark*, Ms. 9/1695, fol. 12v. Musee Conde, Chantilly, France (Giraudon/Art Resource, N.Y.). Used by permission.

Proper 18

Passover Seder Meal in Jewish Tradition, © 1994 Corel Corporation. All rights reserved. Used by permission.

Meichel Pressman, *The Seder*, 1950, watercolor on paper, gift of Dr. Henry Pressman, Jewish Museum, New York, N.Y. (Art Resource, N.Y.). Used by permission.

Ken Heyman, *The Nigerian Railsplitter*, 1960, as reproduced in *The World Family* (New York: G. P. Putnam, 1983). Used by permission of Black Star.

Proper 19

Shalom of Safed, *The Exodus with the Pillar of Fire*, as reproduced in *Images from the Bible: The Words of Elie Wiesel, the Paintings of Shalom of Safed* (New York: The Overlook Press, 1980), 107. Paintings © 1980 by Shalom of Safed. Used by permission.

William Baziotes, *The Beach*, The Whitney Museum of Art, New York, N.Y. Used by permission.

Proper 20

Film still from *Edward Scissorhands*, © Twentieth Century Fox. Photo provided by Photofest, New York, N.Y. Used by permission.

Stained glass window, *Moses and Manna from Heaven*, Great Malvern Priory, Worcester, Great Britain (Bridgeman/Art Resource, N. Y.). Used by permission.

Ercole de Roberti, *The Israelites Gathering Manna*, The National Gallery, London, England. Used by permission.

Käthe Kollwitz, *Germany's Children Are Hungry! (Deutschlands Kinder Hungern!)*, 1924 lithograph, Rosenwald Collection, National Gallery of Art, Washington, D.C. Used by permission.

Proper 21

Jacob Lawrence, *Harriet and the Promised Land* (New York: Windmill Books, 1968). Copyright © 1968, 1993 Jacob Lawrence. Reprinted by permission of Simon and Schuster Books for Young Readers.

Ainslie Roberts, *The Storyteller*, as reproduced in *Ainslie Roberts and the Dreamtime* (Richmond, Victoria, Australia: J. M. Dent Pty, 1988). Used by permission.

Clark B. Fitz-Gerald, *Altar Screen at St. Mark's Episcopal Church*, New Canaan, Connecticut. Used by permission of the artist.

Proper 22

Fourth grade at St. Francis Xavier School, *Moses Quilt*, 1994, 45 West High Street, Gettysburg PA 17325. Used by permission.

Sorel Etrog, *Moses*, Los Angeles County Museum of Art, Los Angeles, Calif. Used by permission.

Tadao Tanaka, *The Ten Commandments*, as reproduced in *The Bible Through Asian Eyes*, ed. Masao Takenaka and Ron O'Grady (Auckland, New Zealand: Pace Publishing in association with the Asian Christian Art Association, 1991). Used by permission.

Proper 23

Rembrandt Harmensz van Rijn, *Parable of the Unworthy Wedding Guest*, The Albertina Museum, Vienna, Austria. Used by permission.

Diego Rivera, *Dance in Tehuantepec*, private collection. Courtesy of Sotheby's, New York, N.Y. Used by permission.

Proper 24

Titian, *The Tribute Money*, The National Gallery, London, England. Used by permission.

Margaret Bourke-White, *Flood Victims, Louisville, Kentucky*, 1938, in "Margaret Bourke-White," *American Photo* 5, no. 4 (July/August 1994). Used by permission of Time-Life Syndication.

Proper 25

Arthur B. Davies, *Hosannah of the Mountains*, gift of Joseph H. Hirshhorn, 1966, Hirshhorn Museum and Sculpture Garden, Smithsonian Institution, Washington, D.C. Photographed by Lee Stalsworth. Used by permission.

Charles E. Burchfield, *Six O'Clock*, Everson Museum of Art, Syracuse, N.Y. Used by permission.

Rembrandt Harmensz van Rijn, *Holy Family with Cat and Snake* (Jian Chen/Art Resource, N.Y.). Used by permission.

Proper 26

Andrew Wyeth, *Christina's World*, 1948, tempera on gessoed panel, 32 1/4 x 47 3/4″, The Museum of Modern Art, New York, N.Y. Purchase. Photograph © 1996, The Museum of Modern Art. Used by permission.

Manuscript illumination, *Depiction of a Medieval Town (August: Corn Harvest)*, from the *Golf Book of Hours*, MS. Add 24098, f. 25v., British Library, London, England (Bridgeman/Art Resource, N.Y.). Used by permission.

All Saints' Day

Wassily Kandinsky, *Allerheiligen (All Saints')*, Städtische Galerie im Lenbachhaus, Munich, Germany. Used by permission.

Gerard Valcin, *Visit to the Departed*, private collection.

Proper 27

Synthia Saint James, *Visions*, Los Angeles, California. Used by permission of the artist.

Sandra Jorgenson, *Roads*, Elmhurst, Illinois. Used by permission of the artist.

Proper 28

Glen Strock, *Parable of the Talents*, Dixon, New Mexico. Used by permission of the artist.

Carmen Lomas Garza, *Dia de los Muertos/Ofrenda Para Antonio Lomas (Offering to Antonio Lomas)*, Hope College, Holland, Michigan. Used by permission of the artist.

Proper 29

Gislebertus, *Last Judgment*, tympanum and lintel on the west portal, Cathedral St. Lazare, Autun, France (Giraudon/Art Resource, N.Y.). Used by permission.

Aaron Douglas, *The Judgment Day*, as reproduced in James Weldon Johnson, *God's Trombones: Seven Negro Sermons in Verse* (New York: Viking Press, 1927). Used by permission of Viking Penguin, a division of Penguin Books USA, Inc.

Käthe Kollwitz, *Out of Work*, Rosenwald Collection, National Gallery of Art, Washington, D.C. Used by permission.

Seasonal Divider for Advent

Salvador Dali, *Girl Standing at the Window*, 1925, Museo d'Arts Contemporanea, Madrid, Spain (Bridgeman/Art Resource, N.Y.). Used by permission.

Advent 1

Salvador Dali, *Girl Standing at the Window*, 1925, Museo d'Arts Contemporanea, Madrid, Spain (Bridgeman/Art Resource, N.Y.). Used by permission.

Rodolfo Abularach, *Cosimico Azul*, New York, New York. Used by permission of the artist.

Claudio Jimenez, *Festival Cross*, photograph by Dr. Grant LaFarge. Used by permission of que tenaga Buena Mano, P.O. Box 762, Santa Fe NM 87504, 505-982-2912.

Advent 2

Pieter Bruegel, the Elder, *Sermon of St. John the Baptist*, 1566, Szépmùvészeti Múzeum, Budapest, Hungary. Used by permission.

Diego Rivera, *Day of the Dead—The Offering (Dia de Muertos—La ofrenda)*, Court of Fiestas, Level 1, South Wall, Secretaria de Educacion Publica, Mexico City, Mexico (Schalkwijk/Art Resource, N.Y.). Reproduccioin autorizada por el instituto Nacional de Bellas Artes y Literatura. Used by permission.

Advent 3

Minnie Evans, untitled design, Museum at Michigan State University, East Lansing, Mich. Used by permission.

Piet Mondrian, *Red Amaryllis with Blue Background*, watercolor, 18 3/8 x 13″, Sidney and Harriet Janis Collection, The Museum of Modern Art, New York, N.Y. Photograph © 1996, The Museum of Modern Art. Used by permission.

Senad Gubelic, *Child with Gun*, as reproduced in *I Dream of Peace: Images of War by Children of Former Yugoslavia*, compiled by UNICEF (New York: HarperCollins Publishers, 1994) 76. Used by permission of HarperCollins Publishers, Inc.

Advent 4

Ethan Hubbard, *Young Woman of Costura, Guatemala*, as reproduced in *Straight to the Heart: Children of the World* (Chelsea, Vt.: Craftsbury Common Books, 1992). Used by permission of the photographer.

Henry O. Tanner, *The Annunciation*, 1898, The W.P. Wilstach Collection, Philadelphia Museum of Art, Philadelphia, Pa. Used by permission.

Paul Gauguin, *Ia Orana Maria (Hail Mary)*, bequest of Sam A. Lewisohn, 1951, The Metropolitan Museum of Art, New York, N.Y. All rights reserved. Used by permission.

Seasonal Divider for Christmas

Carmen Lomas Garza, *Posada (Inn)*, collection of Marina D. Alvarado and Gilbert Mercado, Jr., Los Angeles, Calif. Used by permission of the artist.

Christmas/Nativity

Georges de La Tour, *The Nativity (The New Born)*, Musee des Beaux-Arts, Rennes, France (Giraudon/Art Resource, N.Y.). Used by permission.

Carmen Lomas Garza, *Posada (Inn)*, collection of Marina D. Alvarado and Gilbert Mercado, Jr., Los Angeles, Calif. Used by permission of the artist.

Joseph Stella, *The Crèche (The Holy Manger)*, The Newark Museum, Newark, N.J. Used by permission.

Christmas 1

Rembrandt Harmensz van Rijn, *Presentation of Christ in the Temple*, c. 1627–28, Kunsthalle, Hamburg, Germany (Kavaler/Art Resource, N.Y.). Used by permission.

Michael Freeman, *Shaker Woman*, London, England. Used by permission.

Mev Puleo, *Presentation, Brazil*, St. Louis, Missouri. Used by permission of the photographer.

Christmas 2

Iris Hahs-Hoffstetter, *We Saw His Glory*, as reproduced in Hans-Ruedi Weber, *Immanuel: The Coming of Jesus in Art and the Bible* (Geneva, Switzerland: WCC Publications, 1984), 111. Used by permission of Frau Gunda Graewe and the heirs of Iris Hahs-Hofstetter.

Betty LaDuke, *Oregon: Jason's Journey*, Ashland, Oregon. Used by permission of the artist.

John Giuliani, *Hopi Virgin Mother and Child*, Bridge Building Images, P.O. Box 1048, Burlington VT 05402. Used by permission.

Seasonal Divider for Epiphany and the Season Following

Jan Brueghel, the Elder, *The Adoration of the Kings*, The National Gallery, London, England. Used by permission.

Epiphany

Aaron Douglas, *Rise, Shine for Thy Light Has Come*, Howard University Gallery of Art, Washington, D.C. Used by permission.

Jan Brueghel, the Elder, *The Adoration of the Kings*, The National Gallery, London, England. Used by permission.

Epiphany 1

W. Eugene Smith, *Tomoko in Her Bath*, © Heirs of W. Eugene Smith. Used by permission of Black Star.

John August Swanson, *The River*, serigraph © 1987, Los Angeles, California. Used by permission of the artist.

Epiphany 2

Sir Joshua Reynolds, *The Infant Samuel*, Tate Gallery, London, England (Tate Gallery, London/Art Resource, N.Y.). Used by permission.

Brother Eric de Saussure, *Samuel's Calling*, as reproduced in *Taizé Picture Bible* (Lahr/Schwarzwald, Germany: Verlag Ernst Kaufmann GmbH, 1978). © Ateliers et Presses de Taizé, 71250 Taizé Communauté, France. Used by permission.

Matthew Inglis, *Walls Have Ears*, as reproduced in Bill Hare, *Contemporary Art in Scotland* (New South Wales, Australia: Craftsmen House, 1990). Photograph by Ralph Hughes. Used by permission of Craftsmen House.

Mev Puleo, *Girls Praying*, St. Louis, Missouri. Used by permission of the photographer.

Epiphany 3

Albert Pinkham Ryder, *Jonah*, gift of John Gellatly, National Museum of American Art, Smithsonian Institution (National Museum of American Art, Washington, D.C./Art Resource, N.Y.). Used by permission.

Howard Finster, *Nineveh (Garden Wall)*, Summerville, Georgia. Used by permission of Finster Folk Art.

Paul Kittelson and Olin Calk, *Whale*, steel and window screen, Houston, Texas. Used by permission of the artists.

Epiphany 4

Edvard Munch, *The Scream*, Nasjonalgalleriet, Oslo, Norway. Used by permission.

Linda Post, *Solstice*, R. Michelson Galleries, Northampton, Mass. Used by permission of R. Michelson Galleries.

Healing of the Possessed of an Evil Spirit, detail of *Expulsion of Demons in the Land of Gadarenes*, Hessiches Landesmuseum, Darmstadt, Germany (Erich Lessing/Art Resource, N.Y.). Used by permission.

Epiphany 5

Wilma Rudolph. Used by permission of AP/Wide World Photos.

Cliff Bahnimptewa, *Kwahu (Eagle)*, The Heard Museum, Phoenix, Az. Used by permission.

Ayako Araki, *Migrating Birds*, as reproduced in *The Bible Through Asian Eyes*, ed. Masao Takenaka and Ron O'Grady (Auckland, New Zealand: Pace Publishing in association with the Asian Christian Art Association, 1991). Used by permission.

Proper 1 (Epiphany 6)

Women in Namibia Dancing, Afrapix/Impact Visuals, New York, N.Y. Used by permission.

Cathy Wilcox, *A Proper Little Lady*, by Nette Hilton (New York: Orchard Books, 1989). Used by permission of HarperCollins Publishers (Australia) Pty., Ltd.

Lars Topelman, *Dog and Man Jumping*, Graphistock, New York, N.Y. Used by permission.

Auguste Rodin, *Dancer with Veils (Danseuse aux Voiles)*, Musee Rodin, Paris, France (Giraudon/Art Resource, N.Y.). Used by permission.

Proper 2 (Epiphany 7)

James Watson, *Resurrection Window*, First Lisburn Presbyterian Church, photography by Gordon Gray, F.R.P.S., Belfast, Ireland. Used by permission.

Wilhelm Morgner, *Fields*, Museum Bochum, Bochum, Germany. Used by permission.

Proper 3 (Epiphany 8)

John Perceval, *Christ Dining in Young and Jackson's*, 1947, collection of Helen and Maurice Alther, Melbourne, Australia. Used by permission of the artist.

Paolo Veronese, *The Feast at the House of Levi*, Accademia, Venice, Italy (Cameraphoto/Art Resource, N.Y.). Used by permission.

Transfiguration Sunday

František Kupka, *Mme. Kupka among Verticals*, 1910–11, oil on canvas, Hillman Periodicals Fund, The Museum of Modern Art, New York, N.Y. Photograph © 1996 The Museum of Modern Art. Used by permission.

Raphael, *The Transfiguration*, Pinacoteca, Vatican Museums, Vatican State, Italy (Scala/Art Resource, N.Y.). Used by permission.

Elijah Pierce, *The Transfiguration*, Columbus Museum of Art, Columbus, Ohio. Used by permission.

Seasonal Divider for Lent

Betty LaDuke, *Guatemala: Procession*, Ashland, Oregon. Used by permission of the artist.

Ash Wednesday

Georges de La Tour, *The Penitent Magdalen*, The Metropolitan Museum of Art, New York, N.Y. Used by permission.

Barnett Newman, *First Station*, Jane Meyerhoff Collection, National Gallery of Art, Washington, D.C. Used by permission.

El Posito (*Little Well of Healing Dirt*) at El Sanctuario de Chimayó, Chimayó, New Mexico. Used by permission of the Catholic Archdiocese of Santa Fe.

Lent 1

God's Covenant with Noah, in *Vienna Genesis*, Cod. Theol. Graec 31, page 5, Austrian National Library, Vienna, Austria. Used by permission.

Barbara Reid, *With hoot and squawk and squeak and bark. . . The animals tumbled off the ark*, in *Two by Two* (New York: Scholastic, 1992), 27. © 1992 Barbara Reid. All rights reserved. Reprinted by permission of Scholastic Canada, Ltd.

Lent 2

Barbara Hepworth, *Merryn (Figure)*, 1962, alabaster, gift of Wallace and Wilhemina Holladay, The National Museum of Women in the Arts, Washington, D.C. Used by permission.

Illuminated manuscript, *Abraham Holding in His Lap His Descendants: Jews, Christians, and Muslims*, Bible de Souvigny, Ms 1, f.256, Bibliotheque Municipale, Moulins, France (Giraudon/Art Resource, N.Y.). Used by permission.

Film still from *The Color Purple*, © 1985, Warner Brothers, Inc. Photo provided by Photofest, New York, N.Y. Used by permission.

Lent 3

El Greco, *Cleansing the Temple*, The National Gallery, London, England. Used by permission.

Mev Puleo, *Say No to Drugs*, St. Louis, Missouri. Used by permission of the photographer.

Lent 4

Ding Fang, *Go into Belief*, 1930, as reproduced in *The Bible Through Asian Eyes*, ed. Masao Takenaka and Ron O'Grady (Auckland, New Zealand: Pace Publishing in association with the Asian Christian Art Association, 1991). Used by permission.

Keith Haring, *Altarpiece: The Life of Christ*, currently at the Grace Episcopal Cathedral, San Francisco, California. Used by permission of the Keith Haring Foundation.

Lent 5

Charles White, *The Prophet #1*, Heritage Gallery, Los Angeles, Calif. Used by permission.

Marc Chagall, *Klageleid des Jeremias*, 1956, © ARS, New York, N.Y. Used by permission of ARS.

Palm/Passion Sunday

Eliot Porter, *Christ's Entry into Jerusalem, Riding an Ass*, Church of Ixtepec, Oaxaca, dye transfer print, Eliot Porter Collection, Amon Carter Museum, Fort Worth, Tex. © Amon Carter Museum. Used by permission.

Max Beckmann, *Landscape, Cannes*, 1934, gift of Louise S. Ackerman, San Francisco Museum of Modern Art, San Francisco, Calif. Used by permission.

Betty LaDuke, *Guatemala: Procession*, Ashland, Oregon. Used by permission of the artist.

Holy Thursday

The Last Supper and Washing of Feet, French Psalter, 1260,
The Metropolitan Museum of Art, New York, N.Y.
Used by permission.

Salvador Dali, *The Sacrament of the Last Supper*, Chester Dale Collection,
National Gallery of Art, Washington, D.C. Used by permission.

The Washing of the Feet, Vie de Jesus Mafa, 24 rue de Marechal Joffre,
78000 Versailles, France. All rights reserved. Used by permission.

Good Friday

Stephen Frost, *Crucifix with Antlers*, Pengrove, California. Used by
permission of the artist.

Georgia O'Keeffe, *Black Cross, New Mexico*, Art Institute Purchase Fund,
Art Institute of Chicago, Chicago, Ill. Used by permission.

Giotto di Bondone, *Crucifixion*, Scrovengi Chapel, Padua, Italy (Scala/Art
Resource, N.Y.). Used by permission.

Seasonal Divider for Easter

Frank Wesley, *Easter Morning*, Galloway Collection, as reproduced
in Naomi Wray, *Frank Wesley: Exploring Faith with a Brush*
(Auckland, New Zealand: Pace Publishing, 1993), 38.
Used by permission.

Easter

Frank Wesley, *Easter Morning*, Galloway Collection, as reproduced
in Naomi Wray, *Frank Wesley: Exploring Faith with a Brush*
(Auckland, New Zealand: Pace Publishing, 1993), 38.
Used by permission.

José Clemente Orozco, *The White House*, Instituto Nacional de Bellas
Artes y Literatura, Mexico City, Mexico. Reproduccioin autorizada por el
instituto Nacional de Bellas Artes y Literatura. Used by permission.

Georgia O'Keeffe, *Abstraction—White Rose, III*, The Alfred Stieglitz
Collection, bequest of Georgia O'Keeffe, Art Institute of Chicago,
Chicago, Ill. Used by permission.

Easter 2

Faith Ringgold, *Church Picnic*, painted story quilt, Englewood, New Jersey.
Photo by Gamma I. Used by permission of the artist.

Anna Raimondi, *And It Filled All the House*, Kapaa, Hawaii. Used by
permission of the artist.

Easter 3

Osmond Watson, *Hallelujah*, 1969, The National Gallery of Jamaica,
Kingston, Jamaica. Photograph by Donnette Zacca. Used by permission.

Frederick Varley, *Liberation*, gift of John B. Ridley, donated by the
Ontario Heritage Foundation, Art Gallery of Ontario, Toronto, Canada.
Used by permission of the F. H. Varley Estate/Mrs. Donald McKay.

Easter 4

Michael Tracy, *Cruz: La Pasión*, as reproduced in *The River Pierce:
Sacrifice II, 13.4.90* (San Ygnacio/Houston, Tex.: The River Pierce
Foundation/Rice University Press, 1992), 63. Photograph © Keith Carter.
Used by permission.

Diego Rivera, *The Flower Carrier* (formerly *The Flower Vendor*), Albert M.
Bender Collection, gift of Albert W. Bender in memory of Caroline
Walter, San Francisco Museum of Modern Art, San Francisco, Calif.
Used by permission.

Maurice Sendak, *In the Dumps*, as reproduced in *We Are All in the Dumps
with Jack and Guy* (New York: HarperCollins Publishers, 1993). © 1993 by
Maurice Sendak. Used by permission of HarperCollins Publishers.

Easter 5

Ainslie Roberts, *Laughter at Dawn*, 1976, private collection of
Basil Sellars. Used by permission.

Robert Lentz, *Tree of Life*, Bridge Building Images, P.O. Box 1048,
Burlington VT 05402. Used by permission.

Kimiyoshi Endo, *Vine and Branches*, as reproduced in Maren C. Tirabassi
and Kathy Wonson Eddy, *Gifts of Many Cultures: Worship Resources for the
Global Community* (Cleveland, Ohio: United Church Press, 1995), 69.
Used by permission of the artist.

Easter 6

James Chapin, *Ruby Green Sings*, Norton Gallery of Art, West Palm
Beach, Fla. Used by permission of the James Chapin Estate.

Georges Seurat, *Bathers at Asnières*, The National Gallery,
London, England (Erich Lessing/Art Resource, N.Y.).
Used by permission.

Easter 7

All May Be One, United Church of Christ National Headquarters, Cleveland, Ohio. Used by permission.

George Tooker, *Embrace of Peace*, Hartland, Vermont. Used by permission of the artist.

The Peace Line in Belfast, Pacemaker Press International, Ltd., Belfast, N. Ireland. Used by permission.

Seasonal Divider for Pentecost (Cycle B)

Beauford Delaney, *Can Fire in the Park*, National Museum of American Art, Washington, D.C. (National Museum of American Art, Washington D.C./Art Resource, N.Y.). Used by permission.

Pentecost

Betty LaDuke, *Africa: Market Day Dreams*, Ashland, Oregon. Used by permission of the artist.

Beauford Delaney, *Can Fire in the Park*, National Museum of American Art, Washington, D.C. (National Museum of American Art, Washington, D.C./ Art Resource, N.Y.). Used by permission.

Trinity Sunday (Pentecost 1)

Manuscript illumination, *Vision of Isaiah*, c. 1000, Staatsbibliothek Bamberg, Bamberg, Germany. Used by permission.

Westminster Abbey, as reproduced in *Westminster Abbey: A Pictorial Guide and Souvenir* (Norwich, England: Jarrold Publishing), 6. Used by permission.

Proper 4

Ben Shahn, *Beatitude*, 1952, private collection. Used by permission of VAGA.

M. C. Escher, *Verbum*, © 1996 M. C. Escher/Cordon Art, Baarn, Holland. All rights reserved. Used by permission of Cordon Art, BV, exclusive worldwide representative of the M. C. Escher Foundation.

Proper 5

Christo and Jeanne-Claude, *Running Fence, Sonomo and Marin Counties, California, 1972–1976*. © Christo, 1976. Photo by Jeanne-Claude. Used by permission of the artists.

Lin Xia Jiang, *Parade of Wind, Series I*, Buffalo, New York. Used by permission of the artist.

Proper 6

Ben Shahn, *The Red Stairway*, St. Louis Art Museum, St. Louis, Mo. © 1996 Estate of Ben Shahn/Licensed by VAGA, New York, N.Y. Used by permission of VAGA.

Ethan Hubbard, *Sisters in the Wind*, as reproduced in *Straight to the Heart: Children of the World* (Chelsea, Vt.: Craftsbury Common Books, 1992). Used by permission of the photographer.

Proper 7

Manuscript illumination, *David and Goliath, Battle of the Israelites and Philistines*, León Bible, Cod. I, 3, Pol 131, Léon Colequta de San Isodora. Ampliaciones y Reproducciones Mas (Arixu Mas). Used by permission of Arixu Mas.

Gian Lorenzo Bernini, *David*, 1623, Galleria Borghese, Rome, Italy (Scala/Art Resource, N.Y.). Used by permission.

Jean Ipoustéguy, *David and Goliath*, 1959, bronze, two figures in four parts, Matthew T. Mellon Foundation, The Museum of Modern Art, New York, N.Y. Photograph © 1996 The Museum of Modern Art. Used by permission.

Martine Barrat/Contact Press Images, *Young Hopeful at Harlem's Artemio Colon Gym*, © 1995 Martine Barrat, New York, New York. Used by permission of Contact Press Images.

Proper 8

Stephen Shames/Matrix, *Mother Clara Hale at 87*, as reproduced in *The African Americans* (New York: Penguin Publishing, 1993). Used by permission of Matrix International, Inc.

Carol Fabricatore, *God's Love We Deliver*, New York, New York. Used by permission of the artist.

Logo, *God's Love We Deliver*, New York, New York. Used by permission of God's Love We Deliver.

Pablo Picasso, *La Soupe*, 1902, Art Gallery of Ontario, Toronto, Canada. © ARS. Used by permission.

Proper 9

Shin Young-Hun, *Outreach of the New Covenant,* as reproduced in *The Bible Through Asian Eyes,* ed. Masao Takenaka and Ron O'Grady (Auckland, New Zealand: Pace Publishing in association with the Asian Christian Art Association, 1991). Used by permission.

Henry O. Tanner, *Disciples Healing the Sick,* Clark-Atlanta University Gallery of Art, Atlanta, Ga. Used by permission.

Proper 10

Richmond Barthé, *Exodus Dance,* National Archives and Records Administration, Still Picture Branch, College Park, Md. Used by permission.

Jan DeBray, *David Dances Before the Ark of the Covenant,* Evansville Museum of Arts and Sciences, Evansville, Ind. Used by permission.

Film still from *Footloose,* © 1984 Paramount Pictures. Photo provided by Photofest, New York, N.Y. Used by permission.

Alan Levenson, *Fancy Dancing,* Tony Stone Images, Chicago, Ill. Used by permission.

Jonathan Green, *The Shout,* Jonathan Green Studios, Inc., Naples, Florida. Used by permission.

Proper 11

Estelle Ishigo, *Boys with Kite,* Special Collections, University Research Library, UCLA, Los Angeles, Calif. Used by permission.

The Wall Came Tumbling Down (New York: Arch Cape Press, 1990), 58. Used by permission of AP/Wide World Photos.

Proper 12

Alemayehu Gizuneh, *Scene X of the Misereor "Hunger Cloth" from Ethiopia,* Aachen, Germany. Used by permission of Misereor Medienproduktion und Vertriebsbesellschaft mbh.

Eucharistic Bread and Fish, catacomb fresco, c. 3rd century, Catacomb of San Callisto, Rome, Italy (Scala/Art Resource, N.Y.). Used by permission.

Jacopo Bassano, *The Feeding of the Five Thousand,* Earl Spencer Collection, Althorp, Northampton, Great Britain (Bridgeman/Art Resource, N.Y.). Used by permission.

Proper 13

Rembrandt Harmensz van Rijn, *Apostle Paul in Prison,* Staatsgalerie, Stuttgart, Germany (Foto Marburg/Art Resource, N.Y.). Used by permission.

Jyoti Sahi, *Jesus Christ—The Life of the World,* Nürnberg, Germany. Used by permission of Missionsprokur, der Oberdeutschen Jesuitenprovinz Sekretariat für Internationale Solidarität.

Proper 14

Dieric Bouts, *Elijah and the Angel,* Altar of the Last Supper, Collegiale, St. Pierre, Louvain, Belgium (Erich Lessing/Art Resource, N.Y.). Used by permission.

Tadao Tanaka, *Elijah and the Crow,* in *The Bible Through Asian Eyes,* ed. Masao Takenaka and Ron O'Grady (Auckland, New Zealand: Pace Publishing in association with the Asian Christian Art Association, 1991). Used by permission.

Proper 15

Jusepe de Ribera, *Ignatius Begins the Spiritual Exercises.* Used by permission of Father Thomas Widner, S.J., Hartnett Jesuit News Service, and Father Richard Blinn.

J. A. Salter, *Taurian Osborne Prays at the New Fellowship Missionary Baptist Church,* Opa Laka, Florida. Used by permission of the photographer.

Judgment of Solomon, lace panel, n.d., Victoria and Albert Museum, London, England (Victoria and Albert Museum/Art Resource, N.Y.). Used by permission.

Proper 16

Jean Fouquet, *Rebuilding of the Temple of Jerusalem Under the Order of Solomon,* Bibliotheque Nationale, Paris, France (Bridgeman/Art Resource, N.Y.). Used by permission.

Henri Matisse, *The Chapel of the Rosary of the Dominicans, Vence, France,* 1948–1951. Photo by Hélène Adant. Used by permission of Soeur Jacques Marie, Chapelle de Vence.

Monastery on Skellig Michael, Bord Failte Photo, Irish Tourist Board. Reproduction rights reserved. Used by permission.

Proper 17

Rick Reinhard, *Base Communities,* Washington, D.C. © Rick Reinhard. Used by permission of the photographer.

Oseola McCarty, Alan S. Weiner/NYT Pictures. Used by permission.

Elijah Pierce, *Obey God and Live,* Columbus Museum of Art, Columbus, Ohio. Used by permission.

Index of Focus Scriptures